Build It!

Make Supercool Models with Your LEGO® Classic Set

VOLUME 2

Jennifer Kemmeter

GRAPHIC ARTS
BOOKS®

Contents

Prehistoric Land

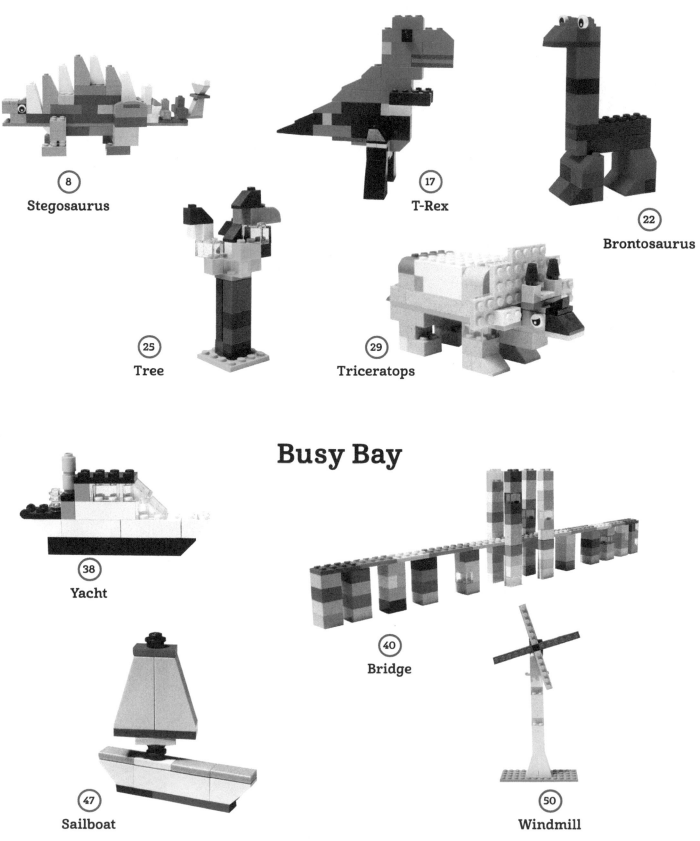

Busy Bay

Desert Scene

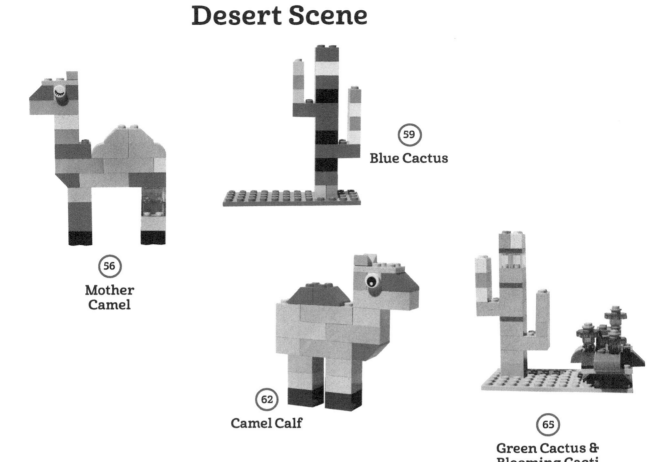

59 Blue Cactus

56 Mother Camel

62 Camel Calf

65 Green Cactus & Blooming Cacti

Seaside Cityscape

75 Airplane

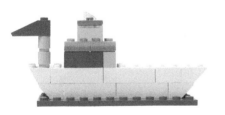

72 Navy Ship

79 Helicopter

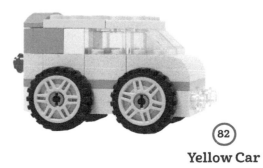

82 Yellow Car

How to Use
This Book

What you will be building.

A photo of what your finished brontosaurus will look like.

Build a Brontosaurus

An illustration of the finished brontosaurus that looks like the pictures in the steps.

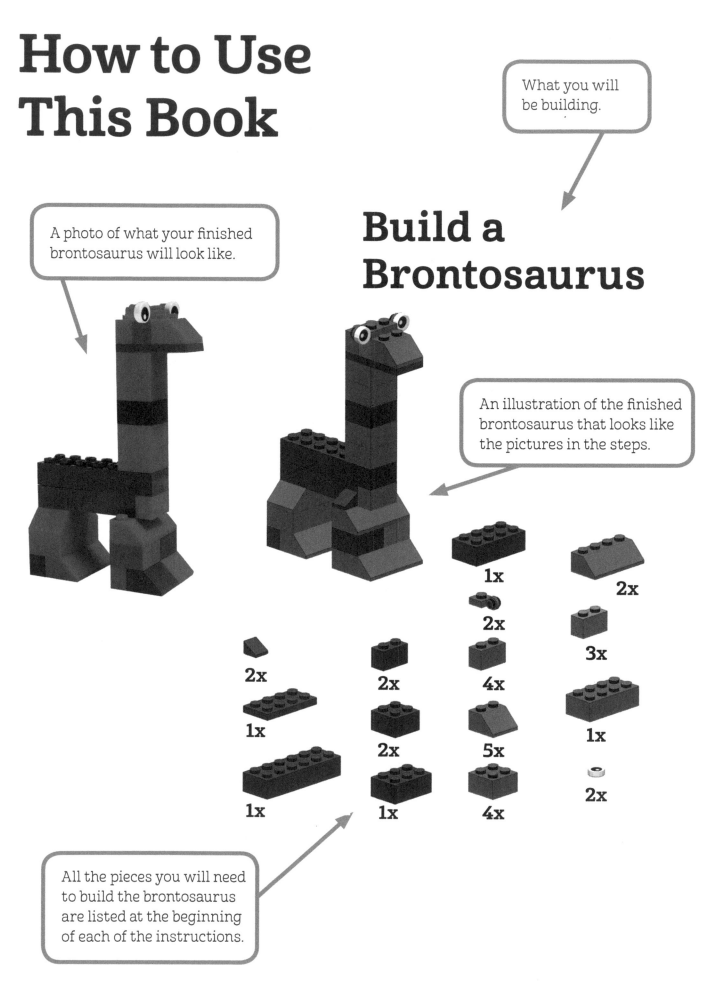

1x

2x

2x

3x

2x

2x

4x

1x

1x

2x

5x

2x

1x

1x

4x

All the pieces you will need to build the brontosaurus are listed at the beginning of each of the instructions.

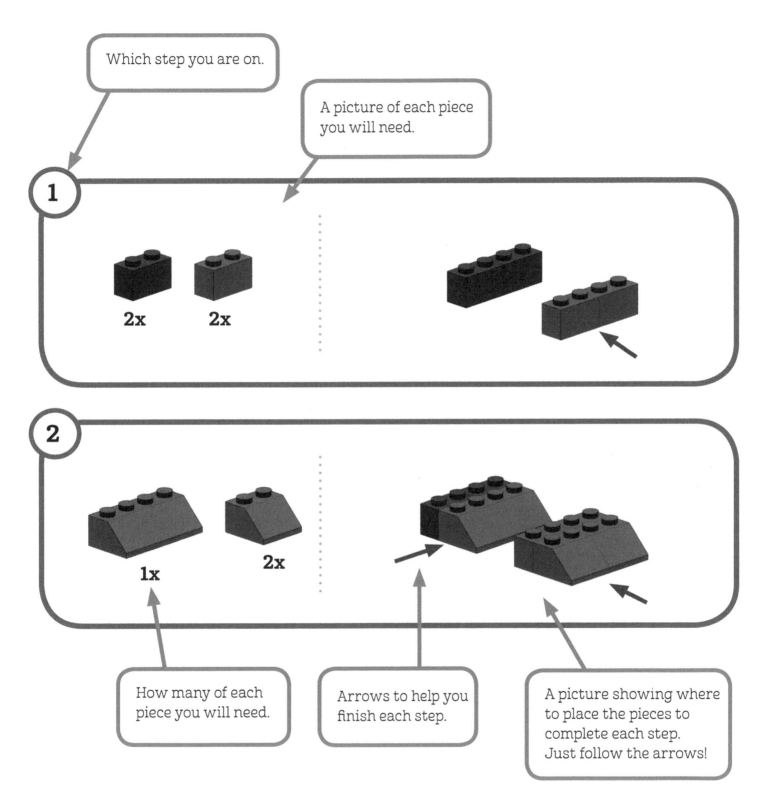

Which step you are on.

A picture of each piece you will need.

1

2x   2x

2

1x   2x

How many of each piece you will need.

Arrows to help you finish each step.

A picture showing where to place the pieces to complete each step. Just follow the arrows!

Prehistoric Land

Triceratops

T-Rex

Tree

Brontosaurus

Stegosaurus

Build a Stegosaurus

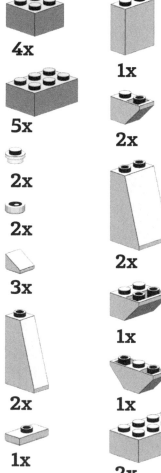

2x

2x

4x

3x

2x

2x

2x

2x

4x

2x

1x

2x

1x

4x

1x

2x

2x

3x

3x

4x

2x

4x

4x

2x

1x

3x

4x

7x

2x

2x

4x

4x

5x

2x

2x

3x

2x

1x

2x

2x

1x

2x

1x

1x

2x

8

1

2x 4x 1x

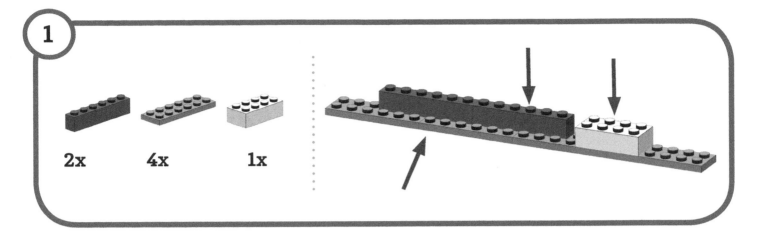

2

2x

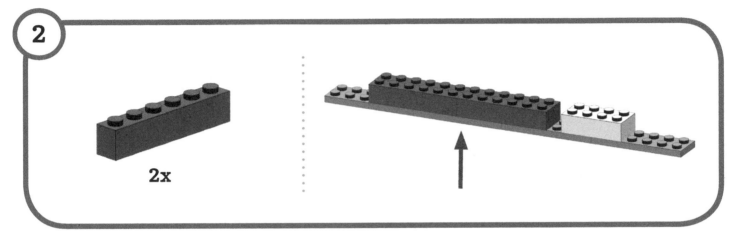

3

1x 2x 2x

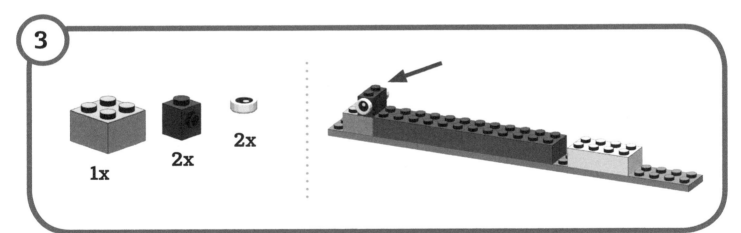

4

1x 1x 2x

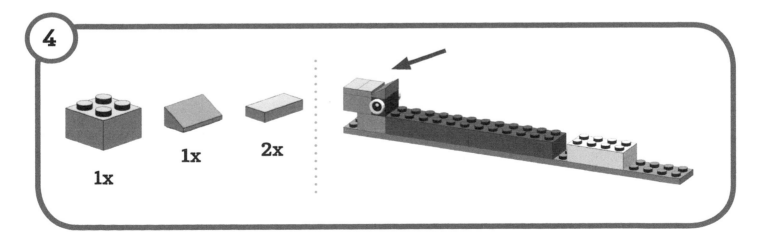

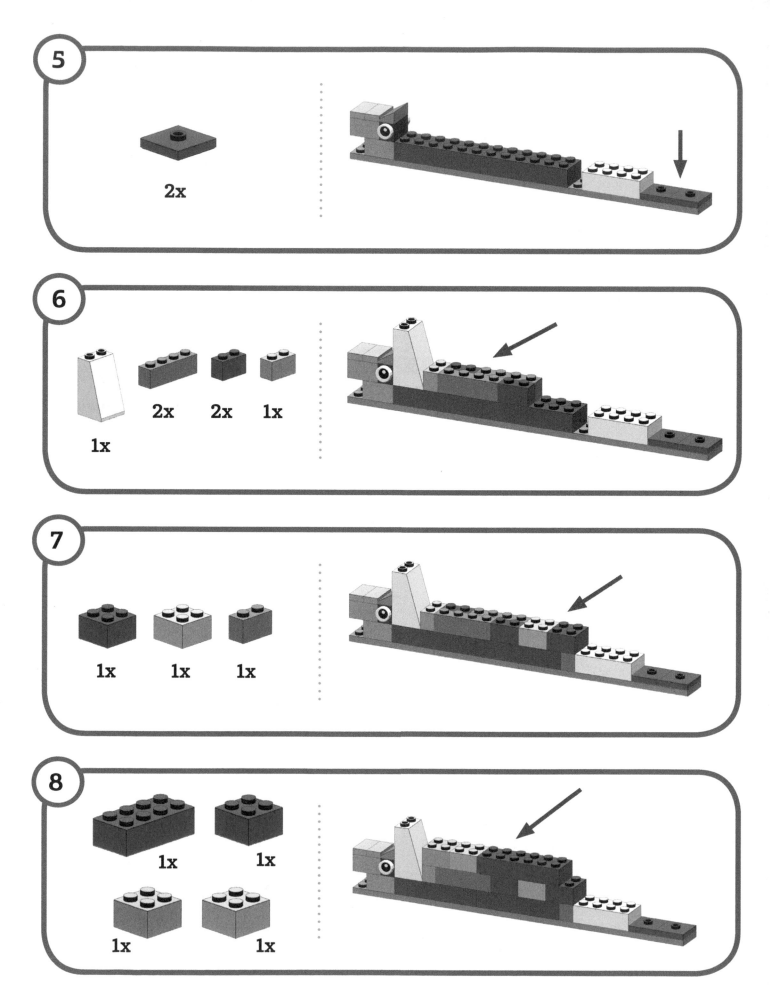

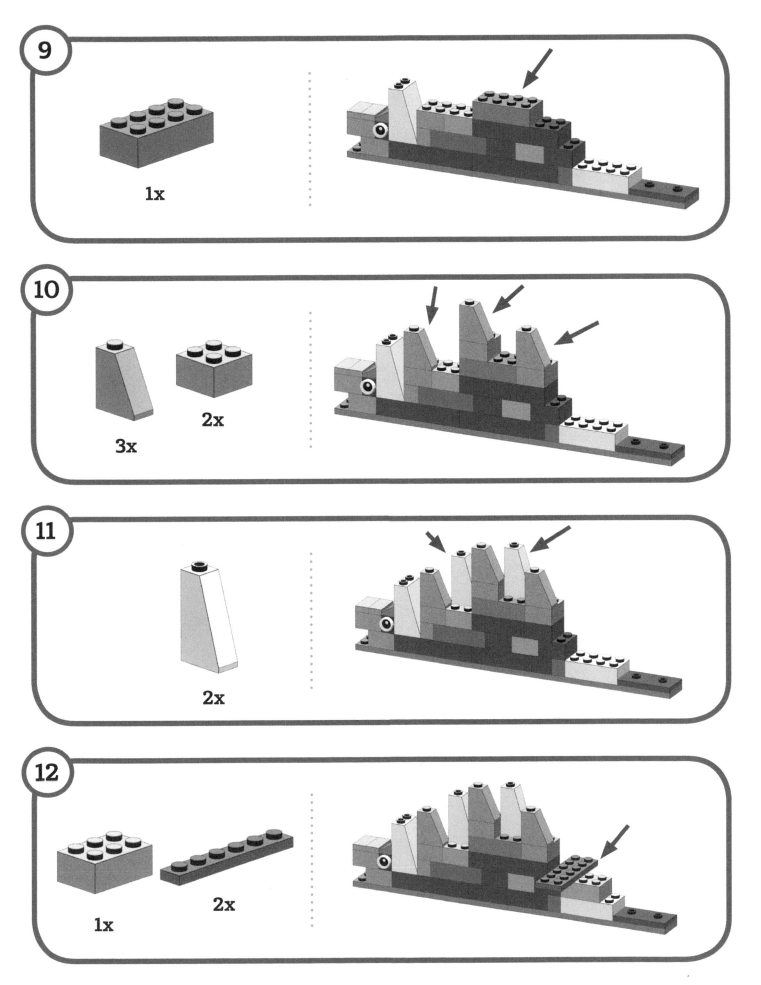

13

1x

1x

1x

2x

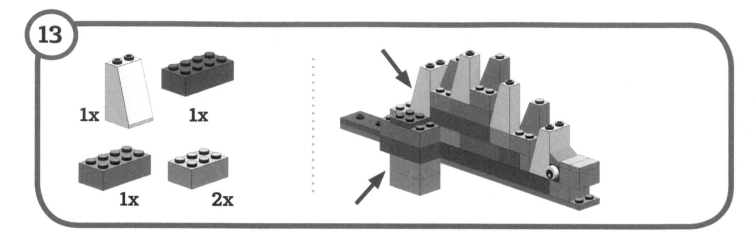

14

1x

1x

2x

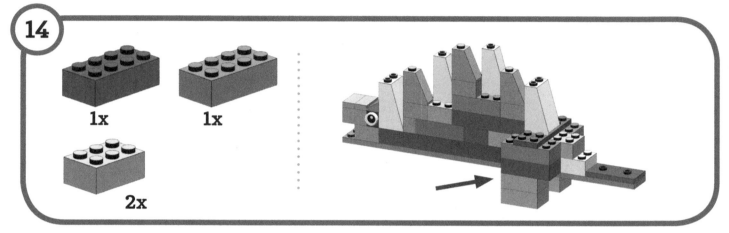

15

1x

1x

1x

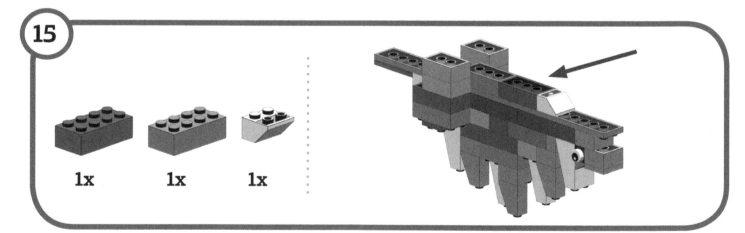

16

2x

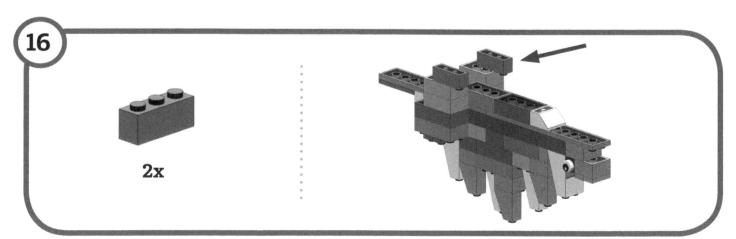

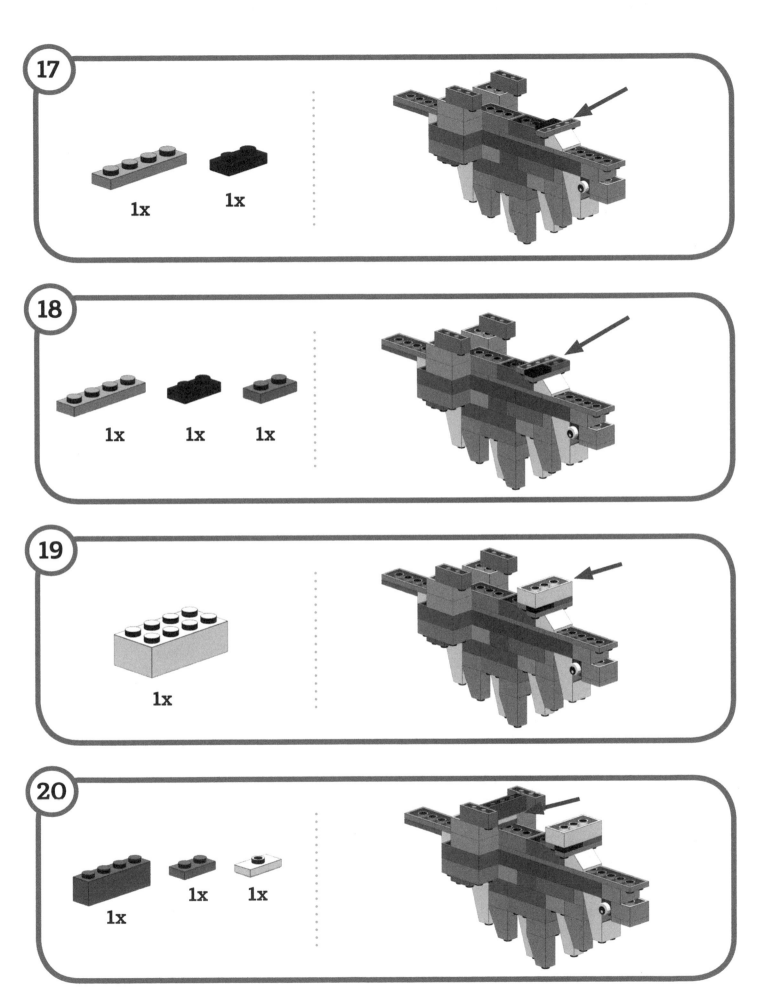

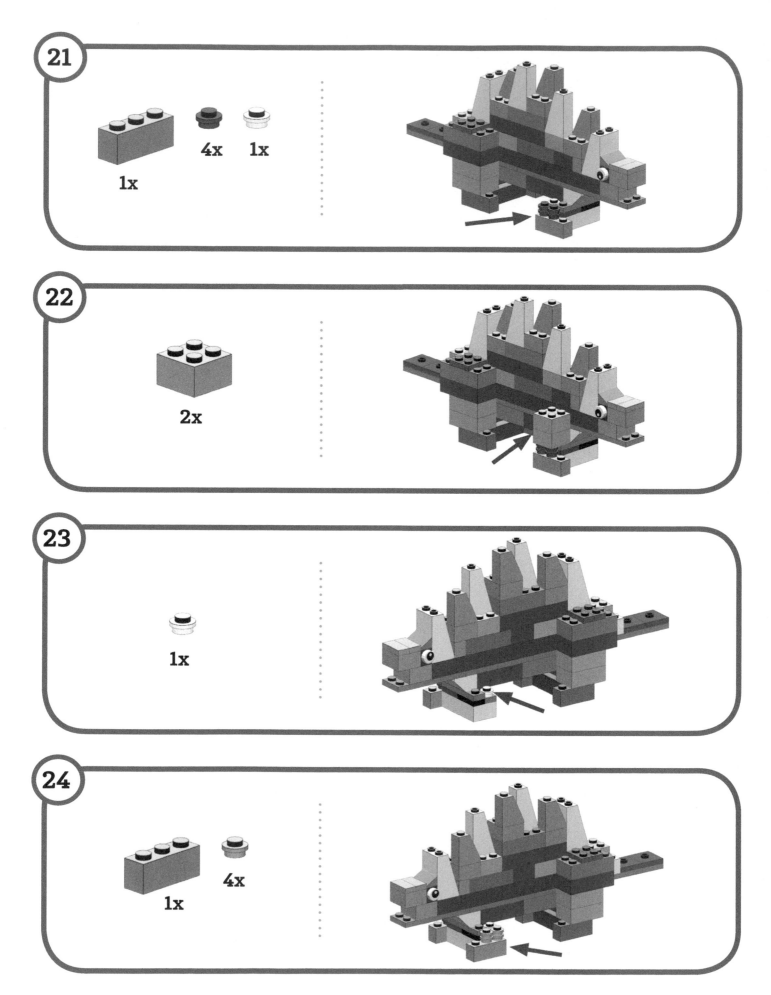

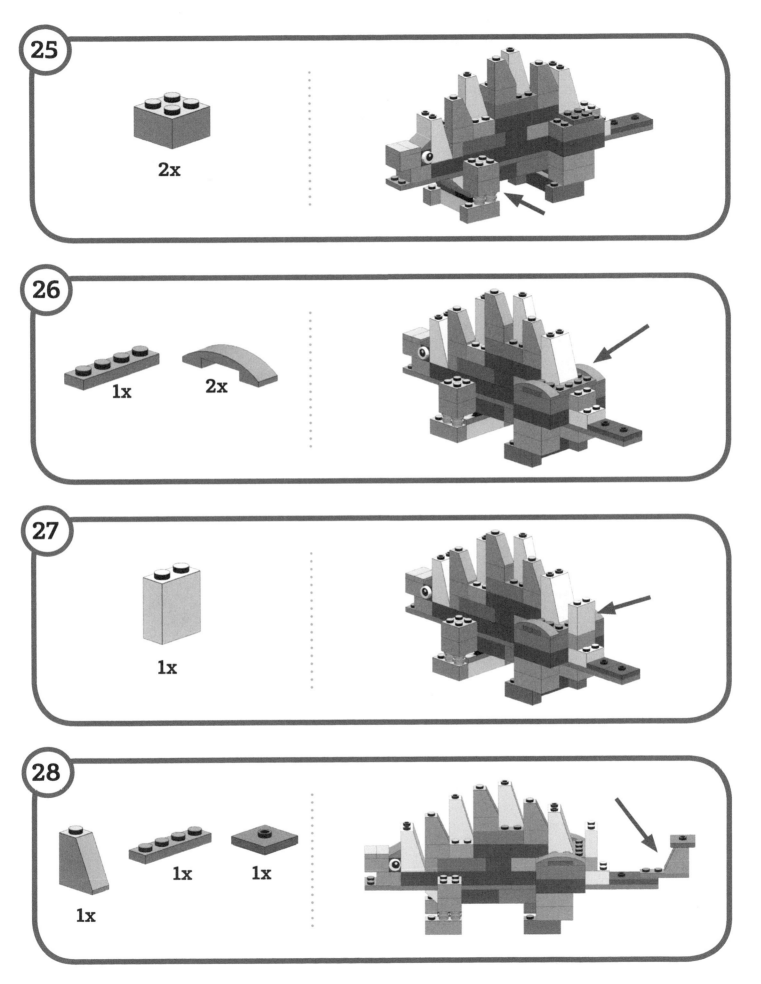

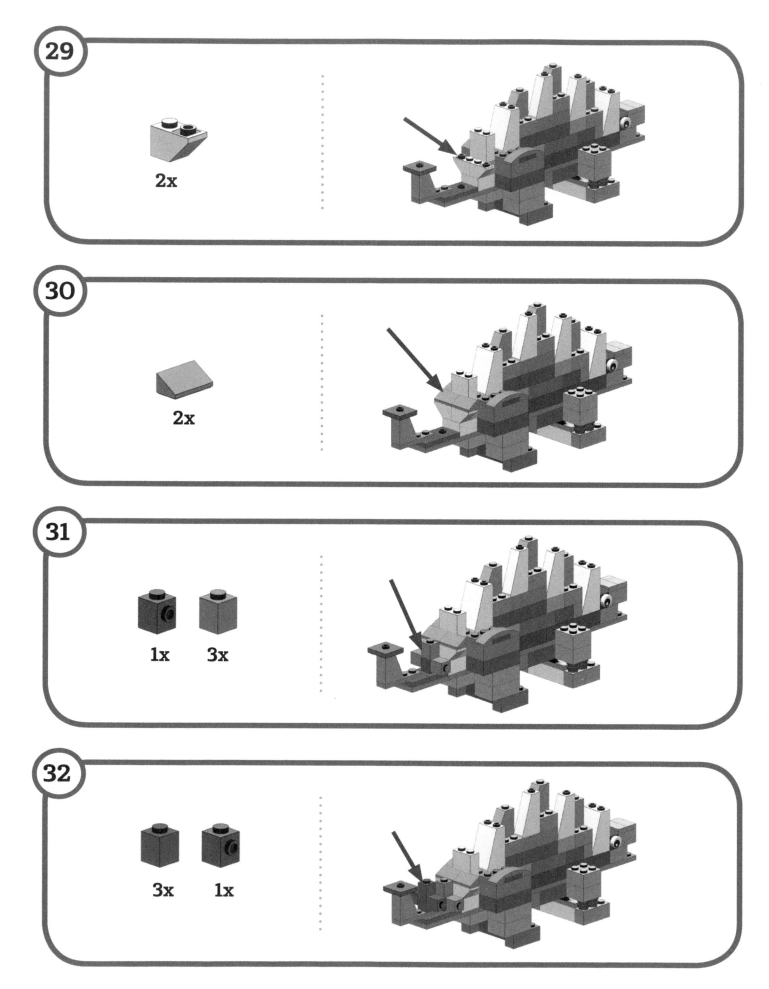

29 2x

30 2x

31 1x 3x

32 3x 1x

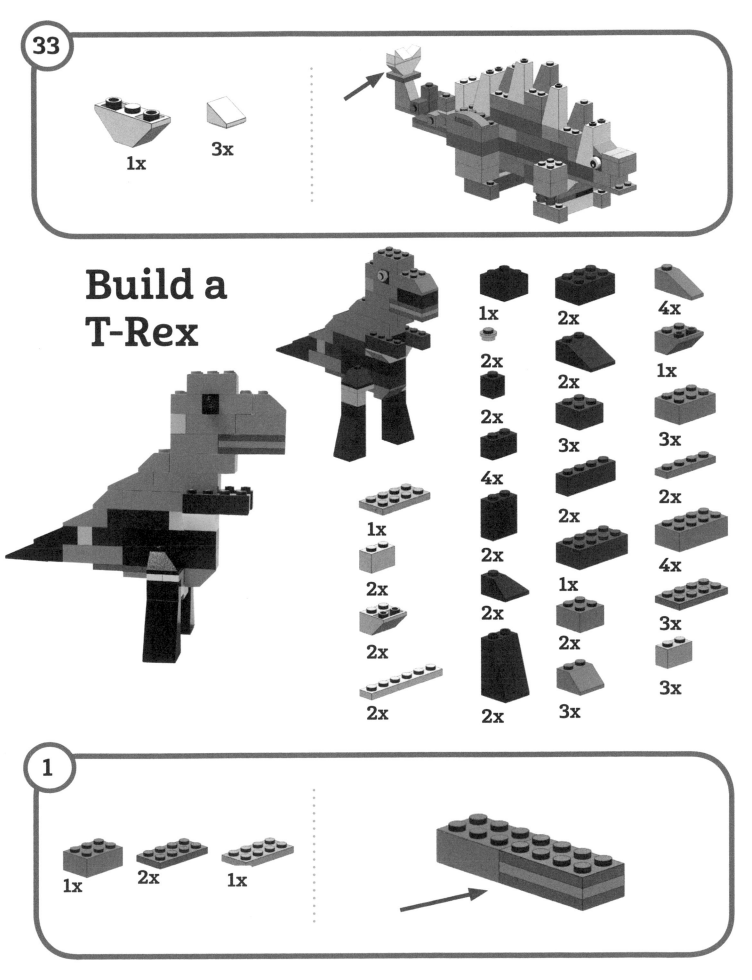

Build a
T-Rex

33

1x   3x

1

1x   2x   1x

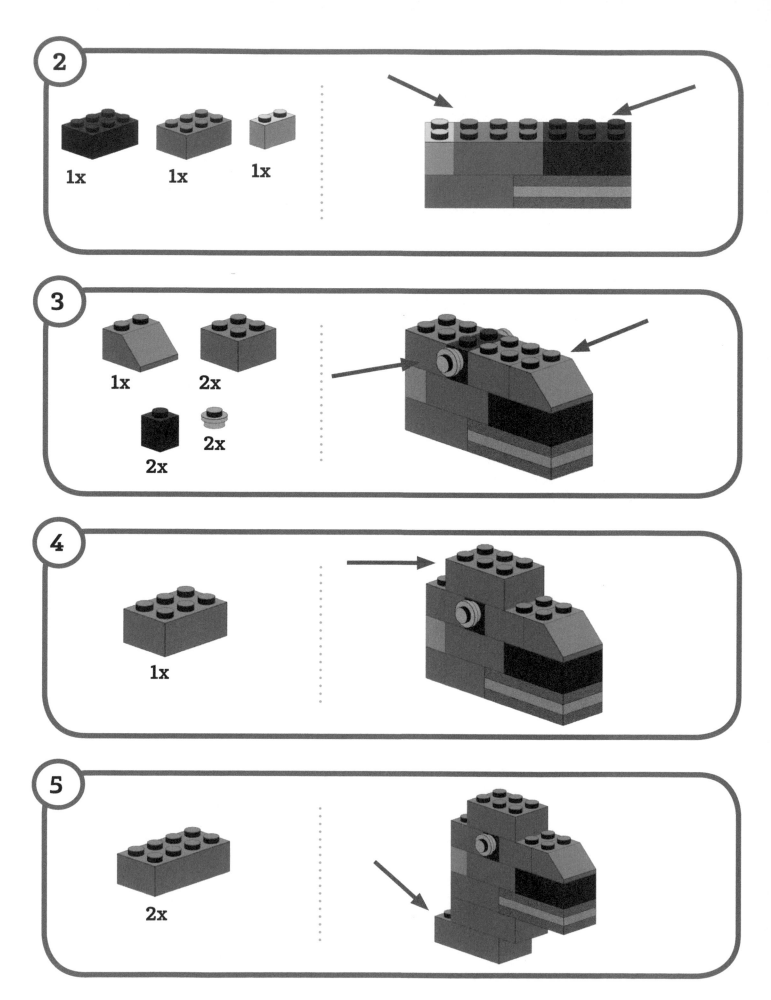

6

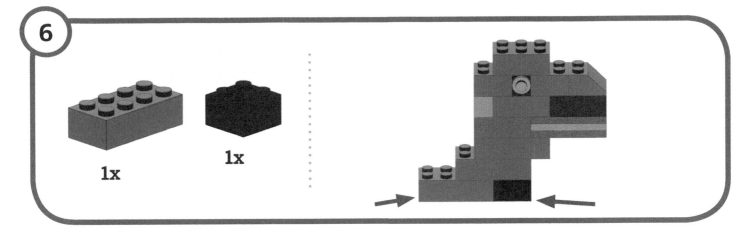

1x **1x**

7

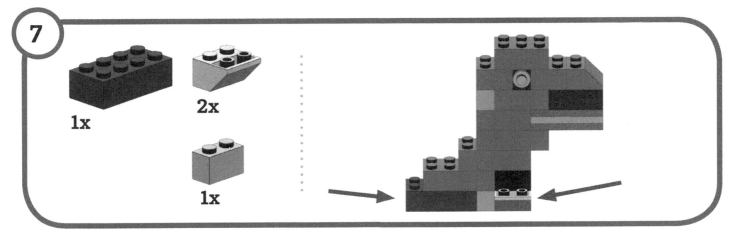

1x **2x**

1x

8

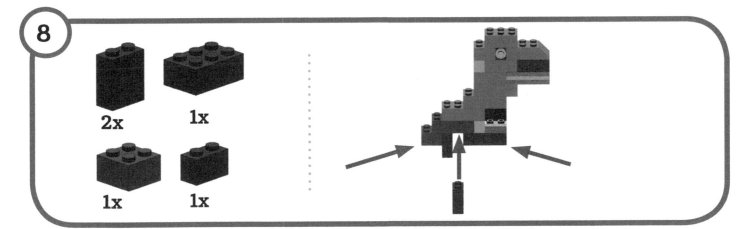

2x **1x**

1x **1x**

9

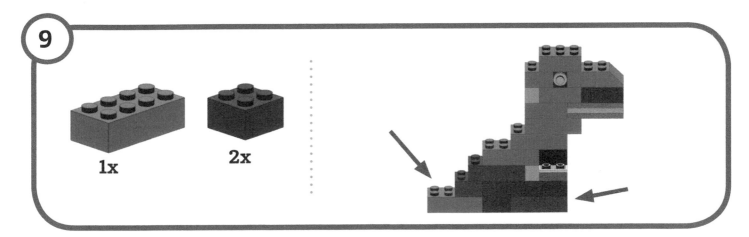

1x **2x**

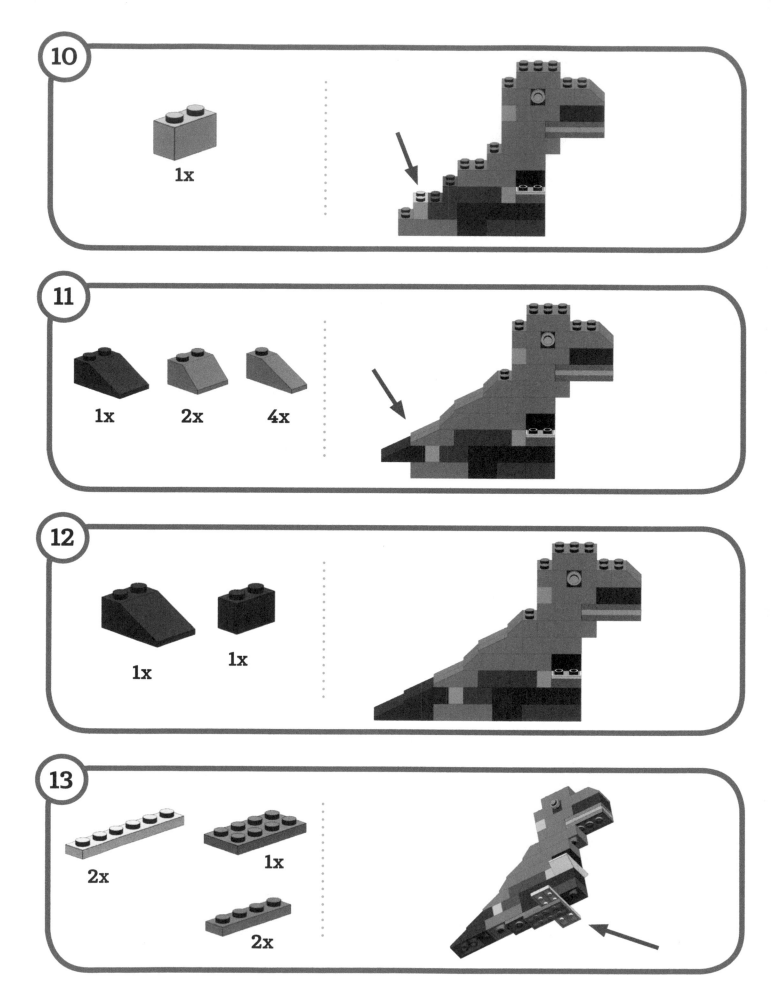

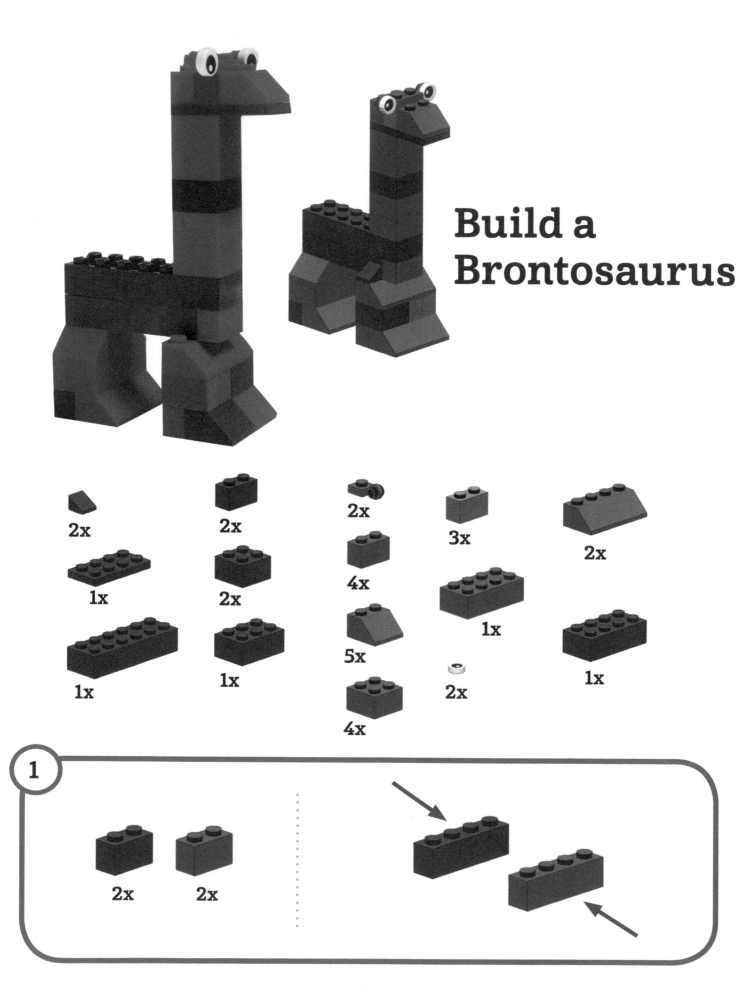

Build a Brontosaurus

1

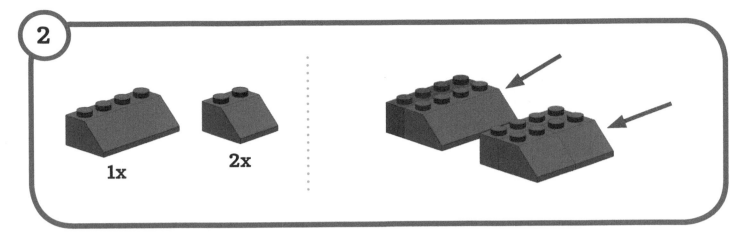

2

1x   2x

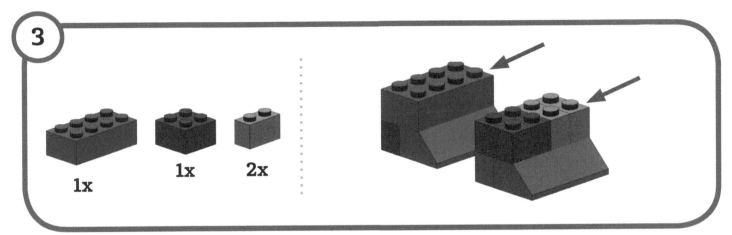

3

1x   1x   2x

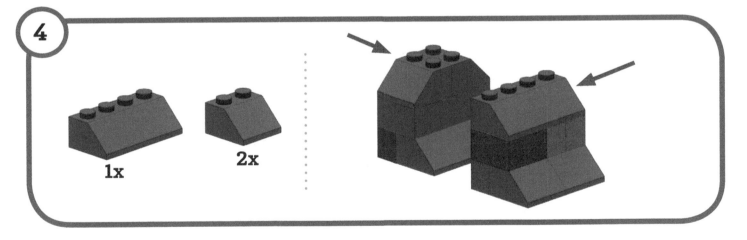

4

1x   2x

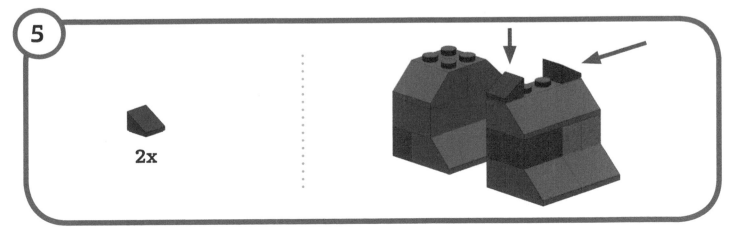

5

2x

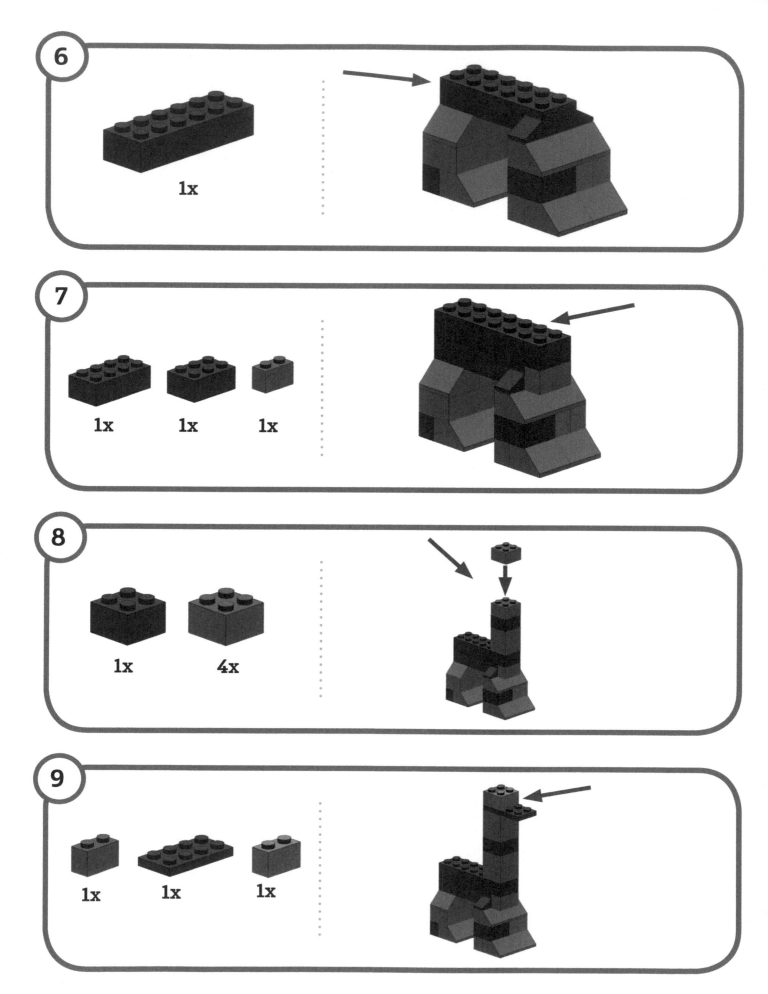

10

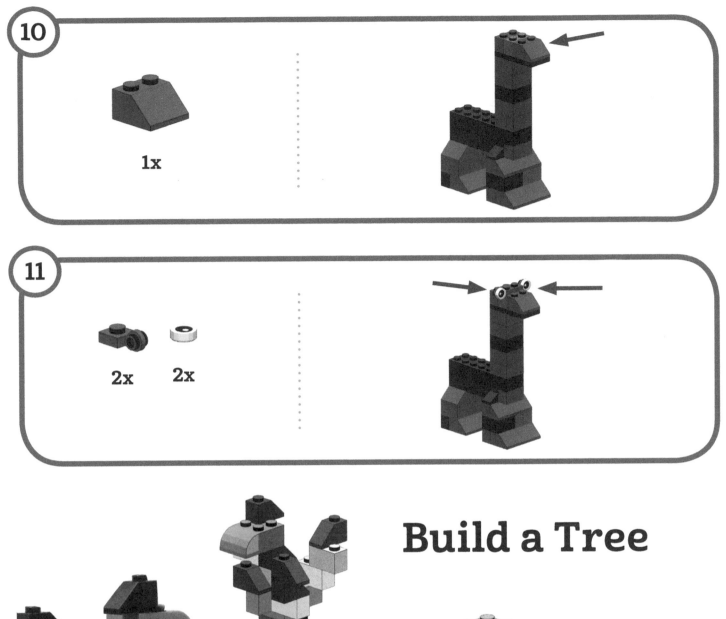

1x

11

2x 2x

Build a Tree

1x

4x

1x

6x

2x

2x

4x 1x 3x

2x

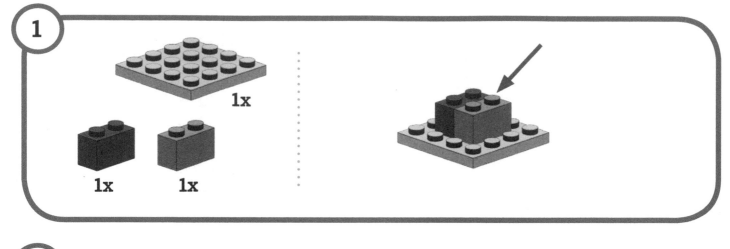

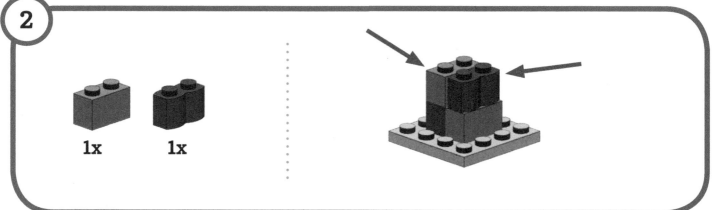

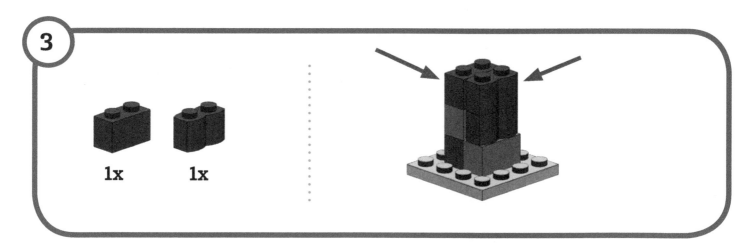

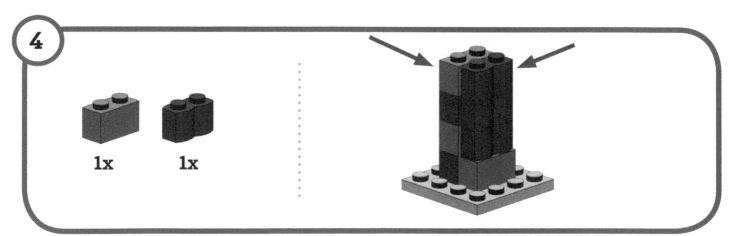

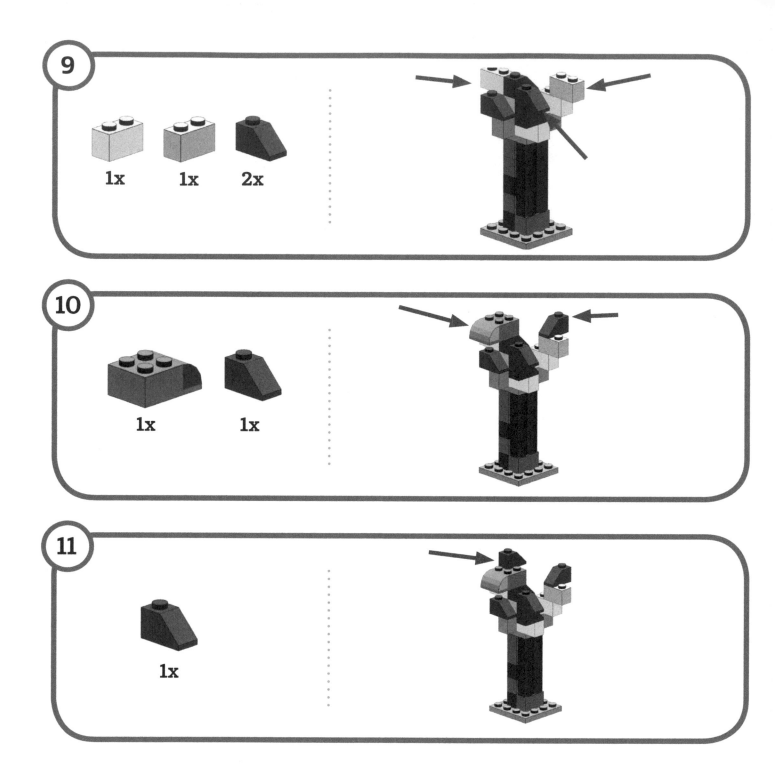

Build a Triceratops

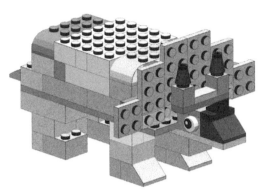

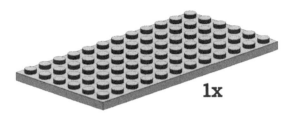
1x

1x

1x

2x

2x

2x

2x

1x

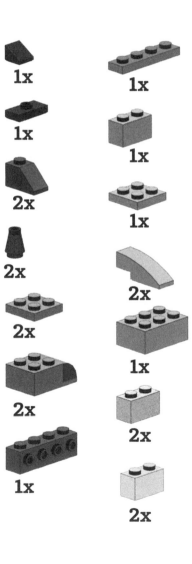

1x

1x

1x

2x

2x

1x

2x

2x

3x

3x

5x

4x

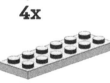
2x

4x

1x

2x

4x

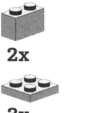
3x

3x

2x

2x

2x

3x

1x

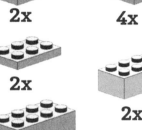
2x

4x

2x

5x

2x

4x

1x

2x

2x

2x

2x

3x

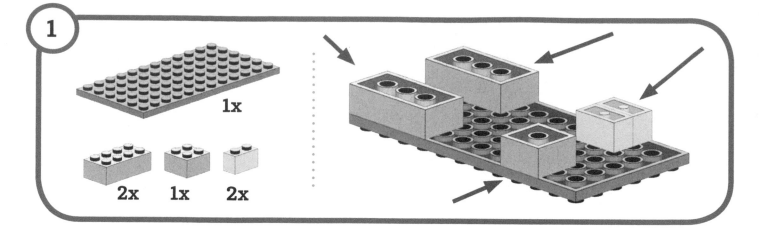

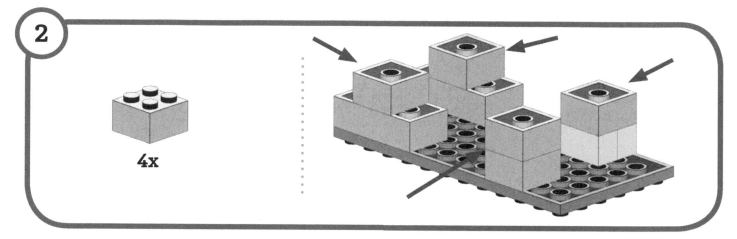

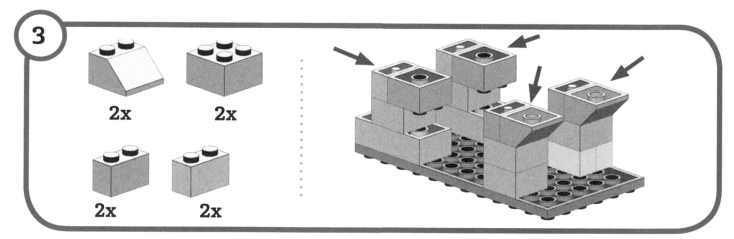

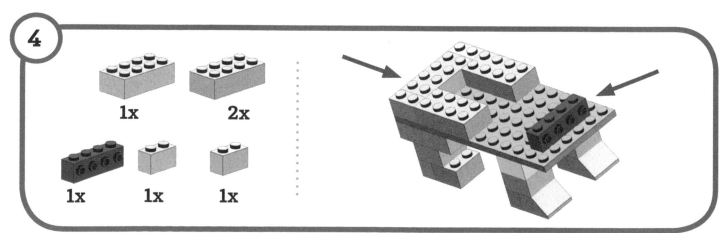

5

2x 2x

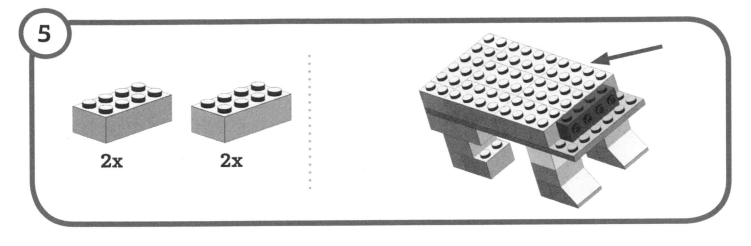

6

1x 1x

7

1x

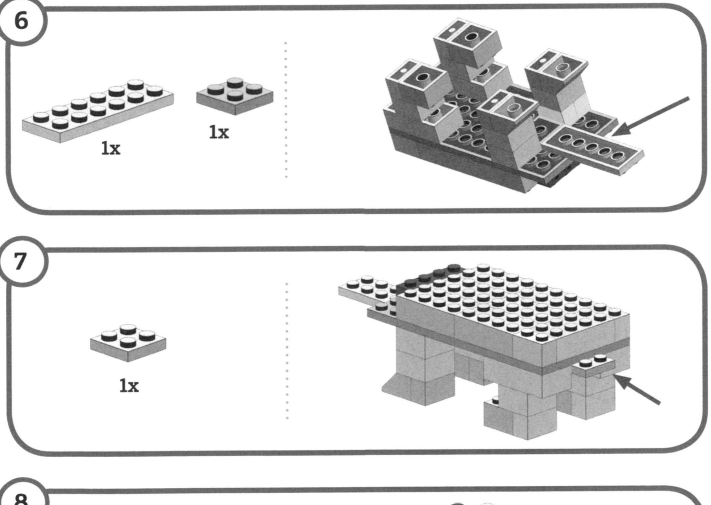

8

2x

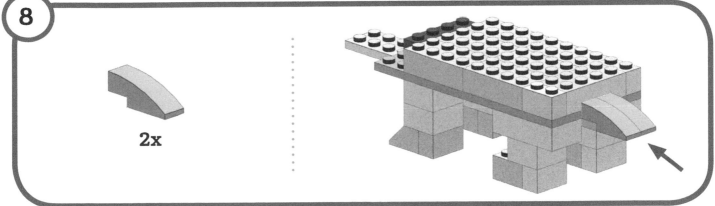

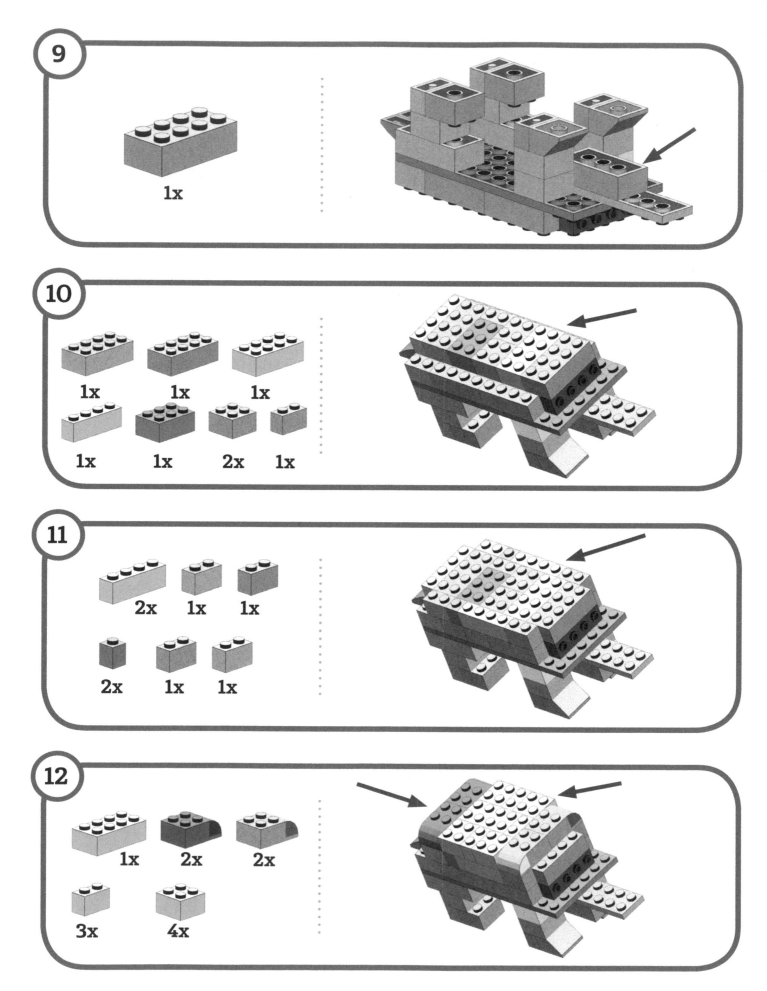

9

1x

10

1x 1x 1x

1x 1x 2x 1x

11

2x 1x 1x

2x 1x 1x

12

1x 2x 2x

3x 4x

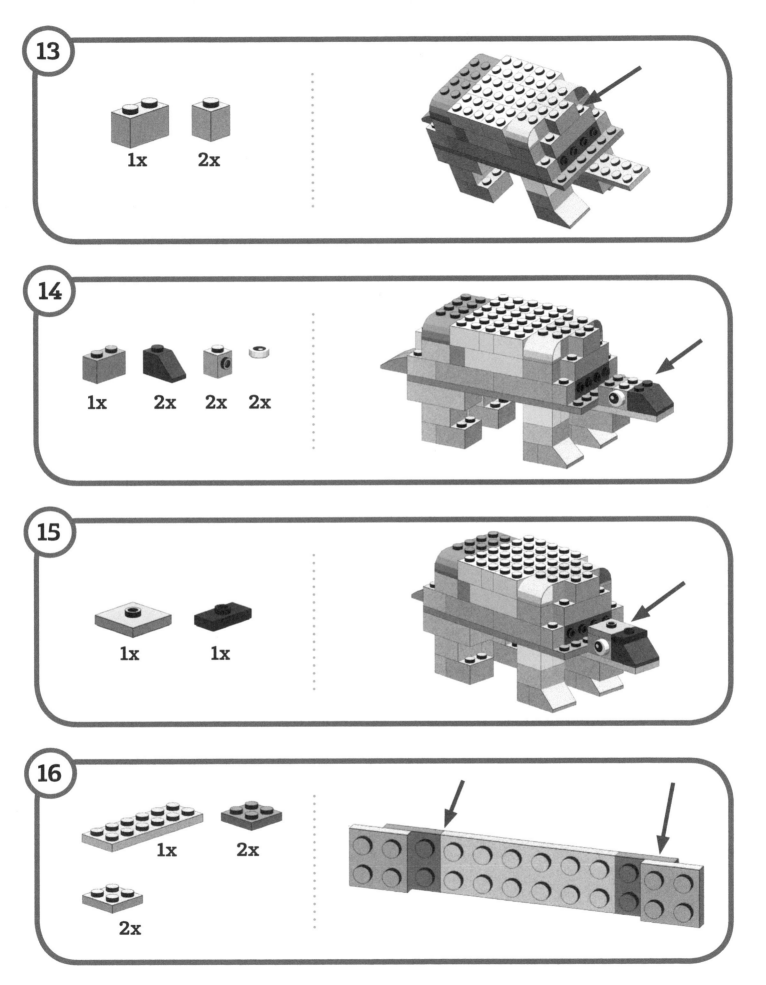

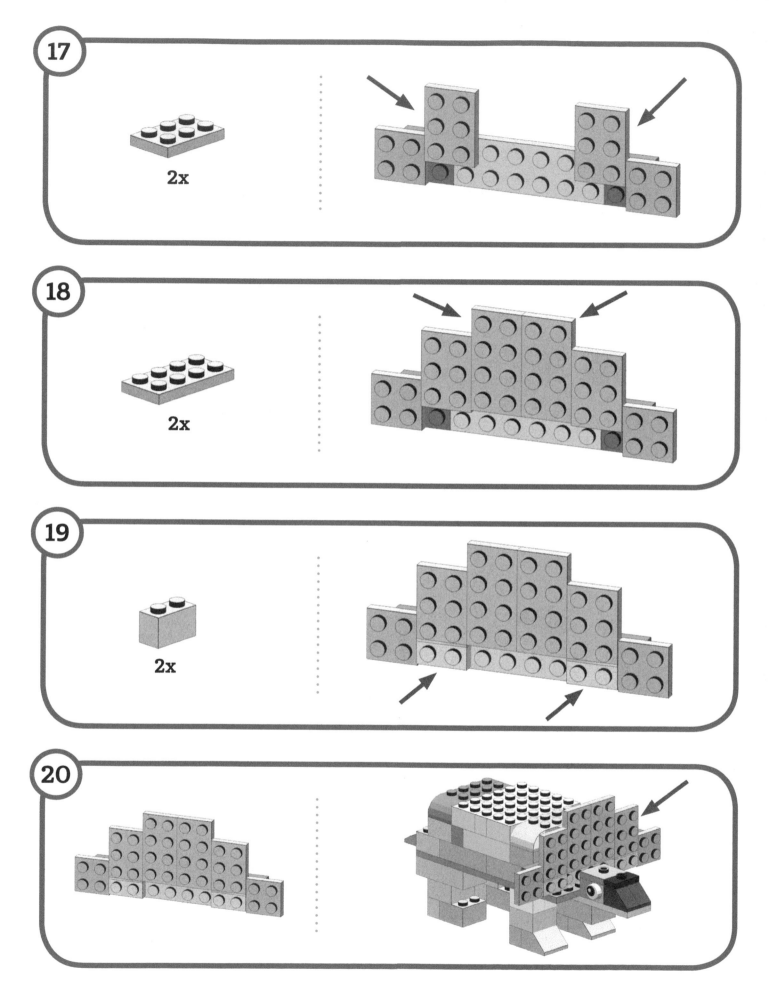

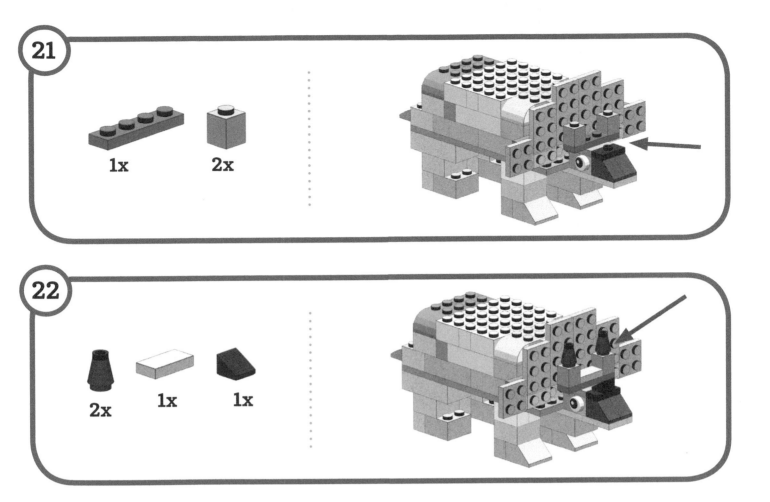

Busy Bay

Windmill

Bridge

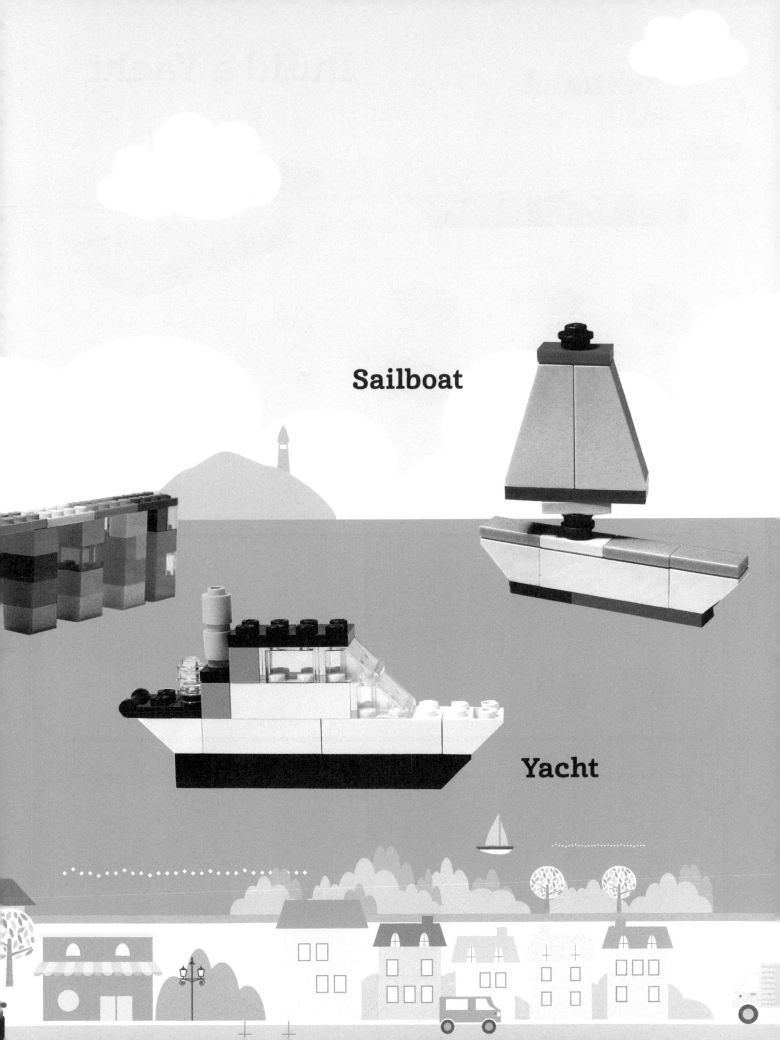

Sailboat

Yacht

Build a Yacht

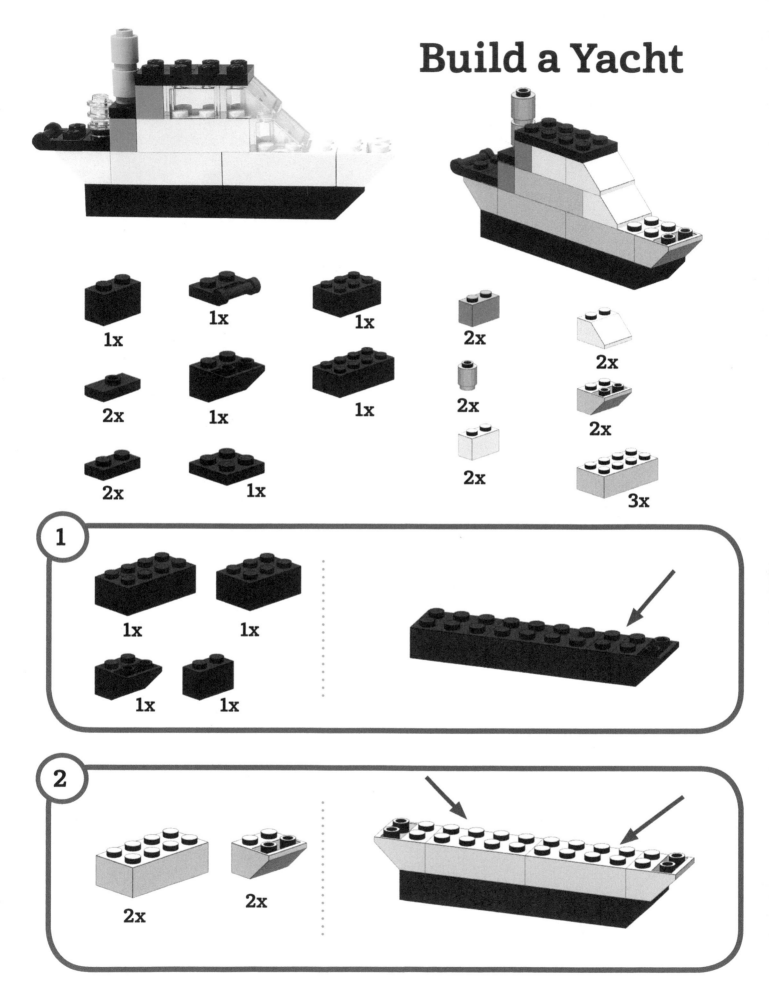

1x

1x

1x

2x

1x

1x

2x

2x

2x

2x

2x

3x

2x

1x

1

1x   1x

1x   1x

2

2x   2x

38

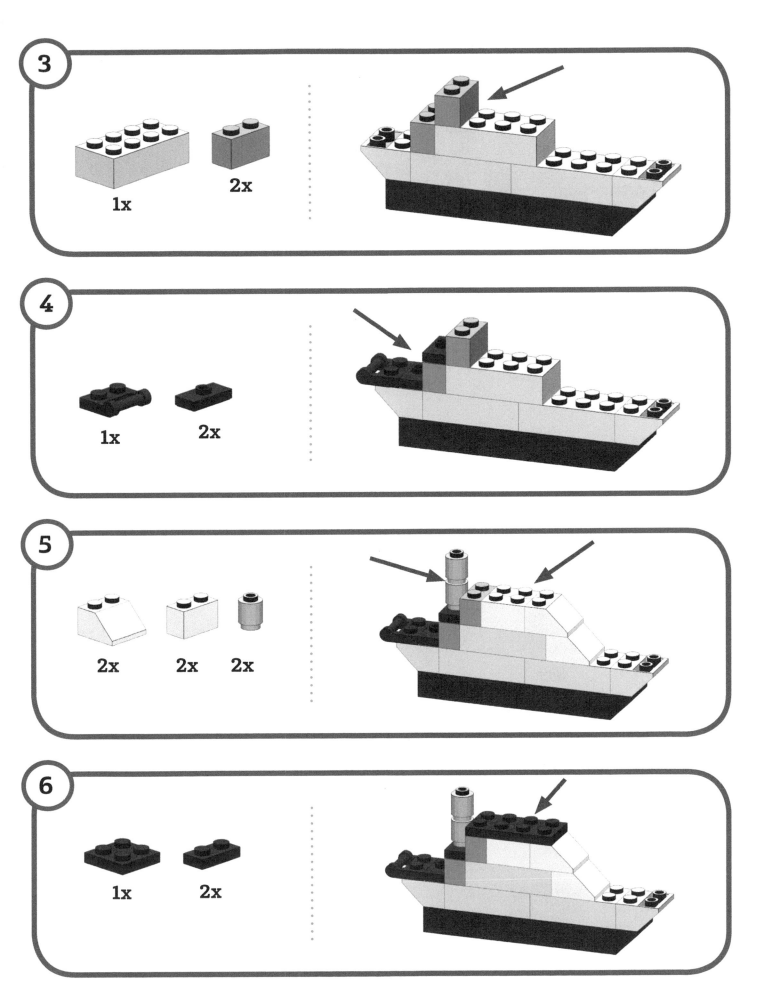

Build a Bridge

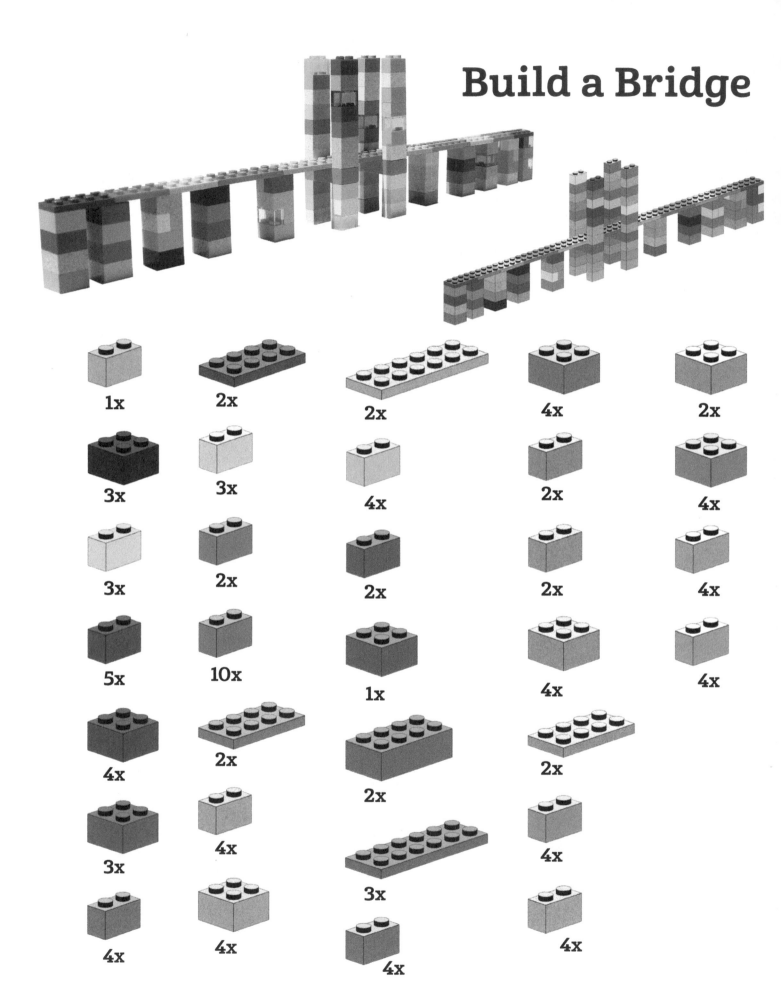

1x

2x

2x

4x

2x

3x

3x

4x

2x

4x

3x

2x

2x

2x

4x

5x

10x

1x

4x

4x

4x

2x

2x

2x

3x

4x

2x

4x

4x

3x

4x

4x

1

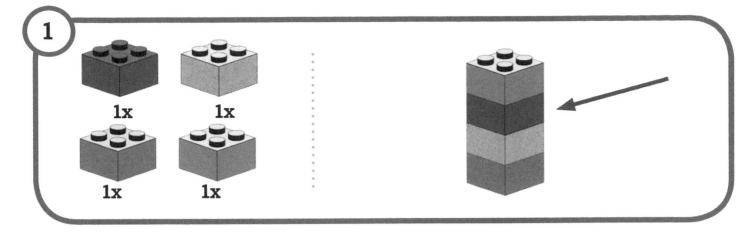

1x 1x
1x 1x

2

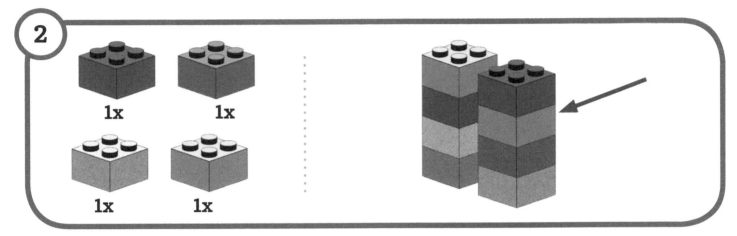

1x 1x
1x 1x

3

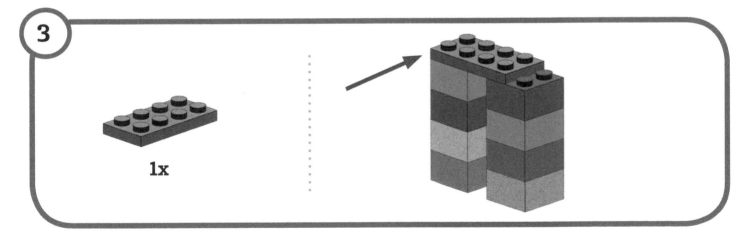

1x

4

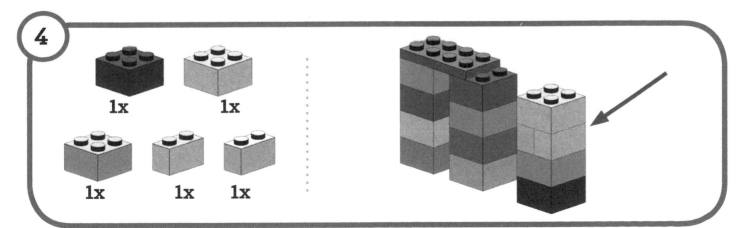

1x 1x
1x 1x 1x

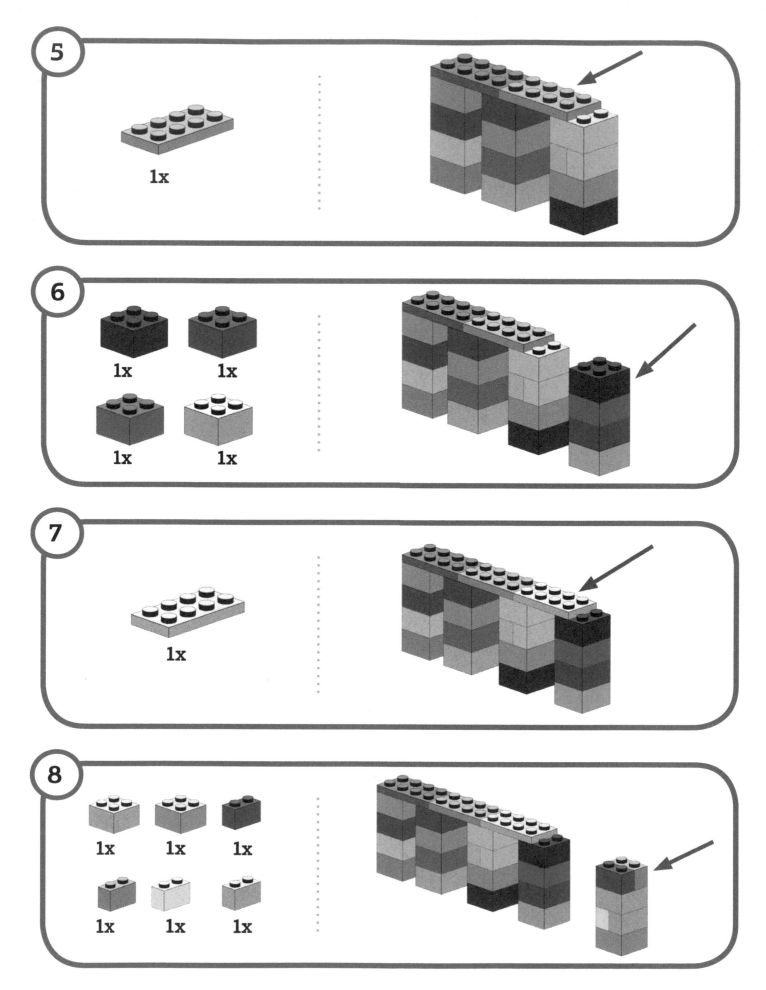

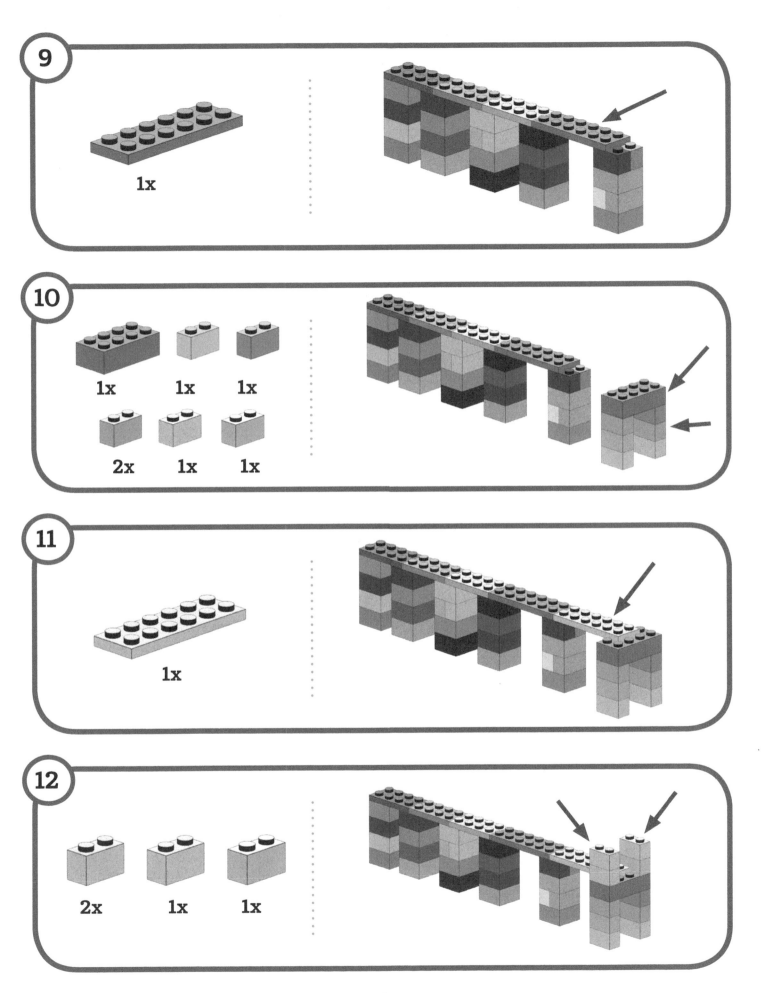

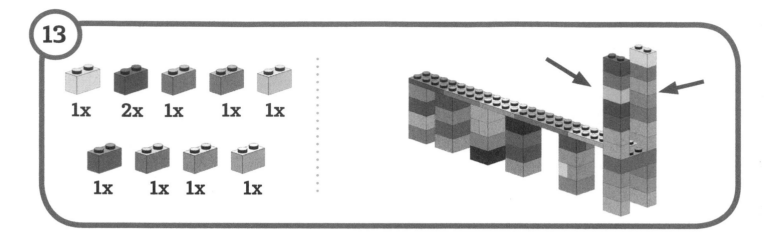

13

1x 2x 1x 1x 1x

1x 1x 1x 1x

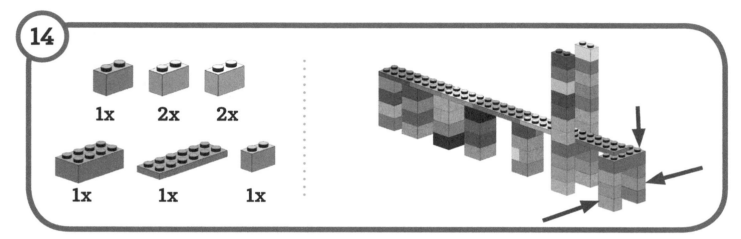

14

1x 2x 2x

1x 1x 1x

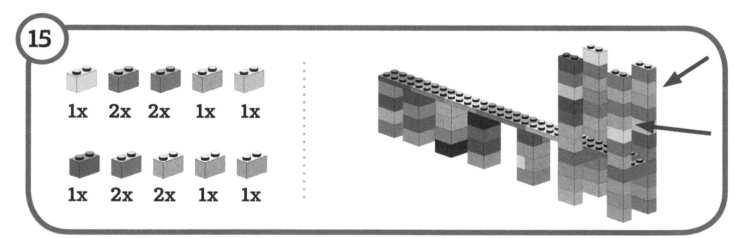

15

1x 2x 2x 1x 1x

1x 2x 2x 1x 1x

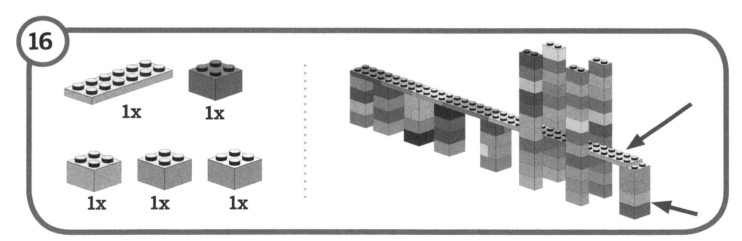

16

1x 1x

1x 1x 1x

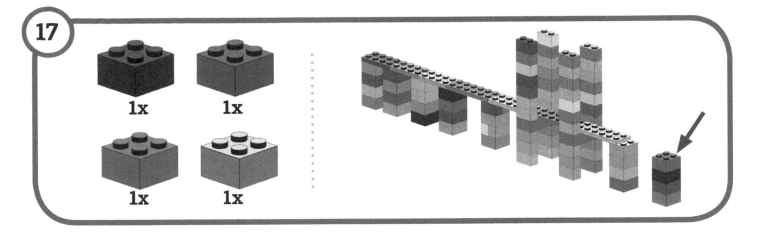

17
1x 1x
1x 1x

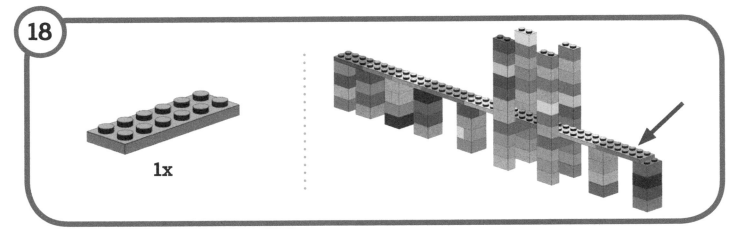

18
1x

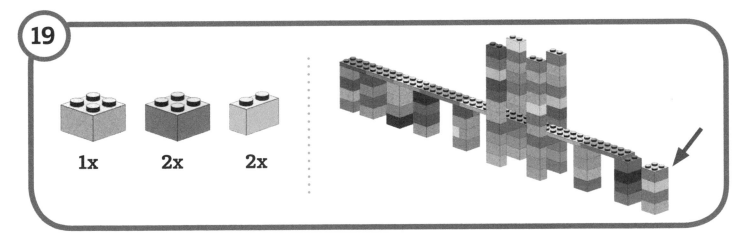

19
1x 2x 2x

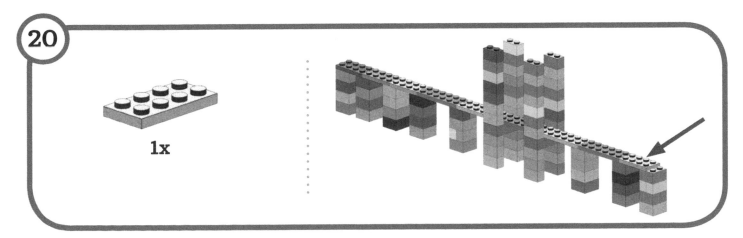

20
1x

21

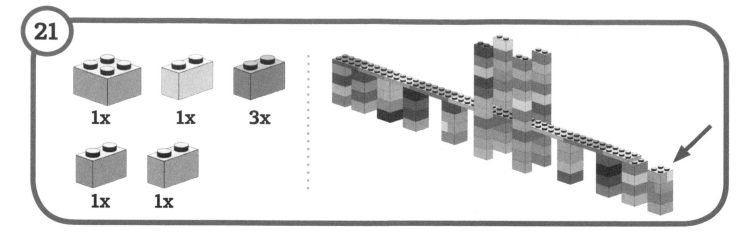

1x **1x** **3x**

1x **1x**

22

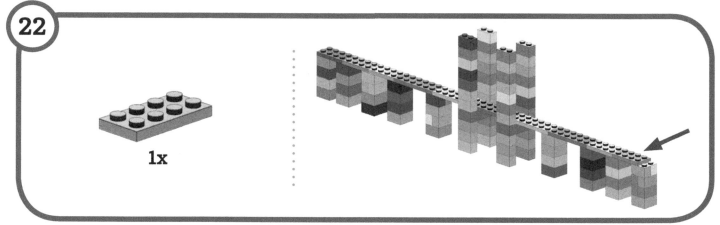

1x

23

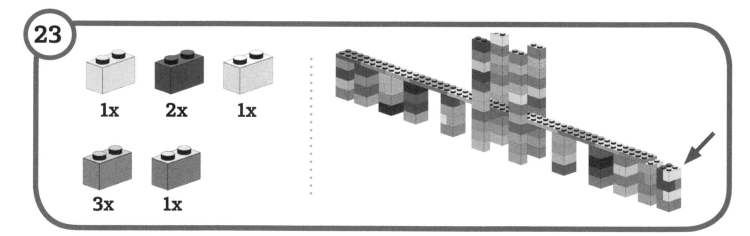

1x **2x** **1x**

3x **1x**

24

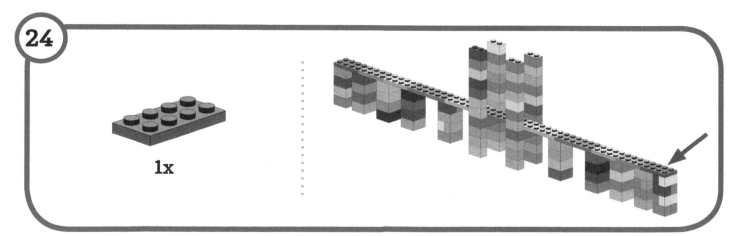

1x

Build a Sailboat

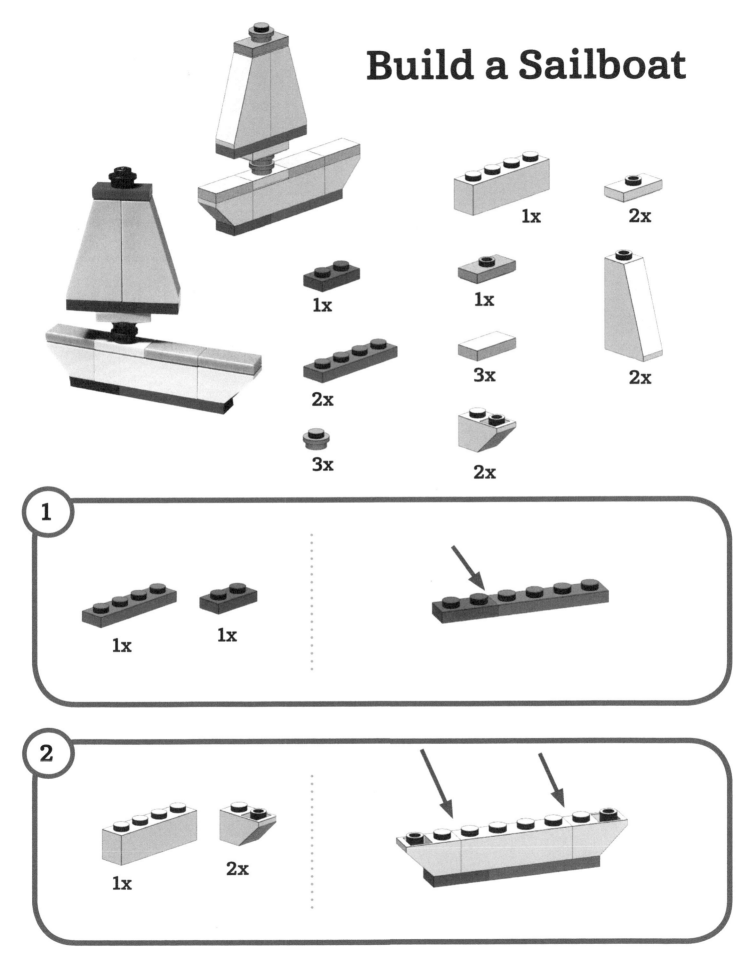

1

1x   1x

2

1x   2x

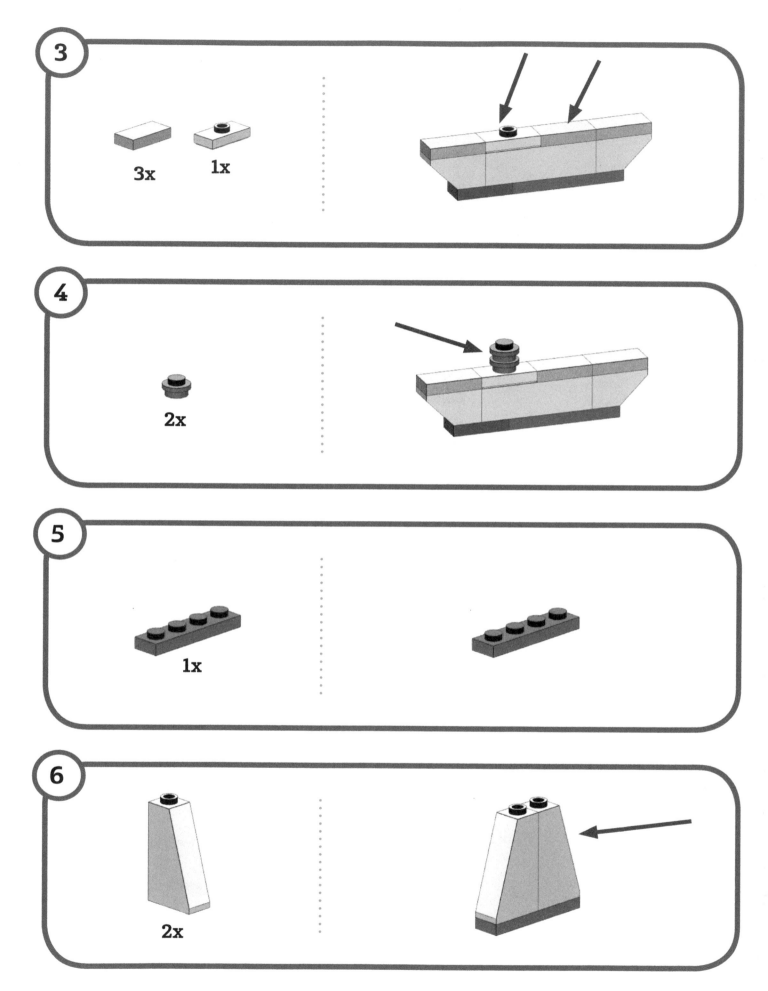

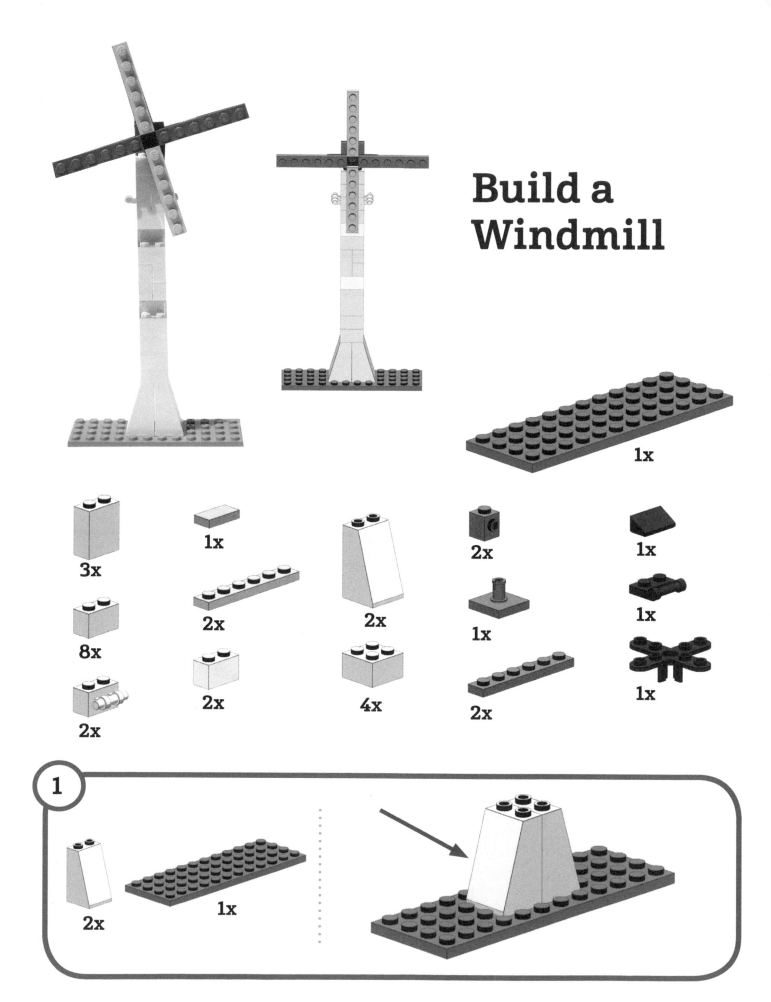

Build a Windmill

1x

3x

1x

8x

2x

2x

2x

2x

2x

4x

1x

2x

1x

1x

1x

1x

1

2x

1x

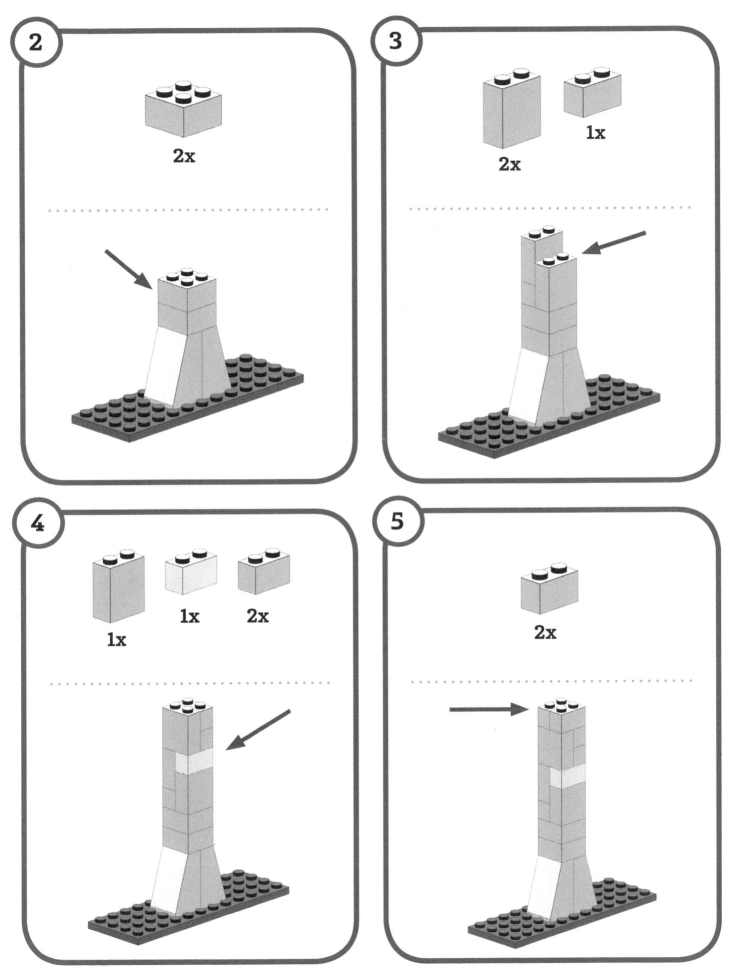

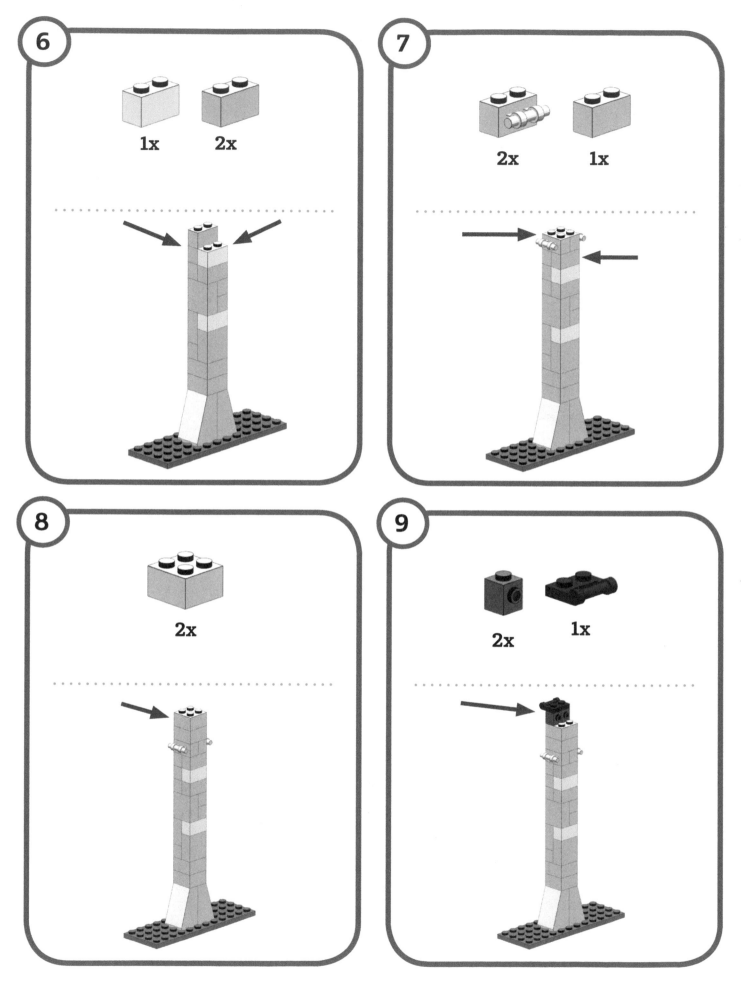

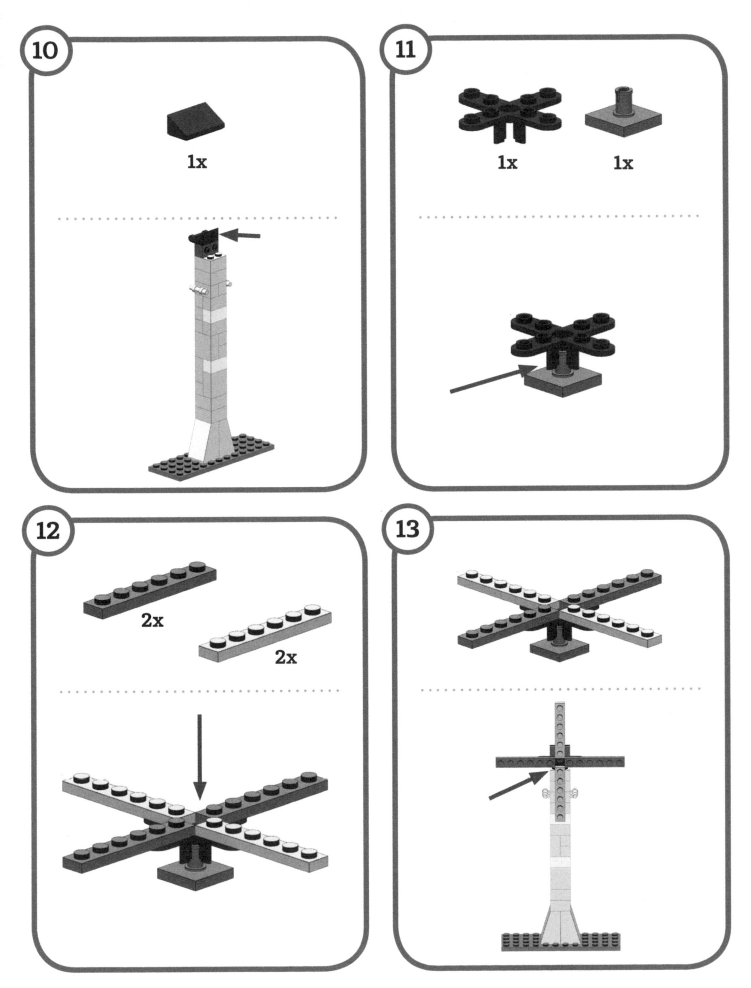

Desert Scene

Camel
Calf

Green Cactus
& Blooming
Cacti

Mother Camel

Blue Cactus

Build a Mother Camel

 4x

 1x

2x

2x

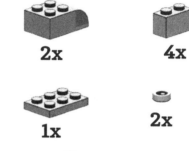 2x

4x

2x

1x

2x

3x

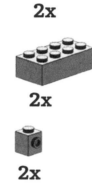 1x

 2x

7x

2x

2x

 2x

2x

1

4x

2

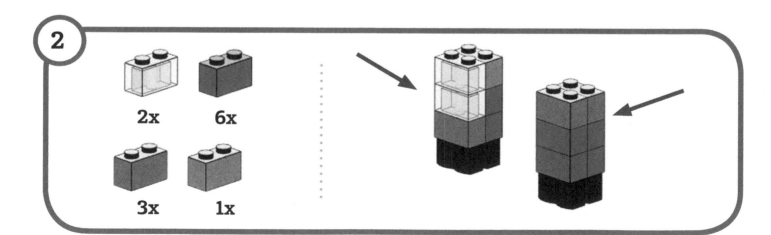

2x   6x

3x   1x

3

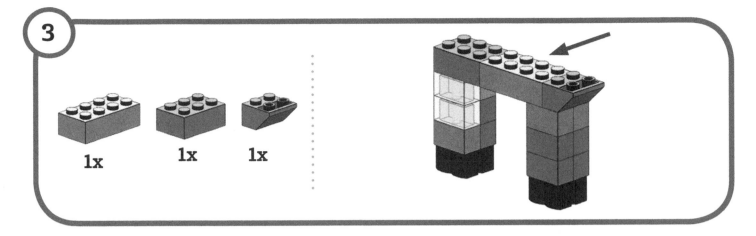

1x 1x 1x

4

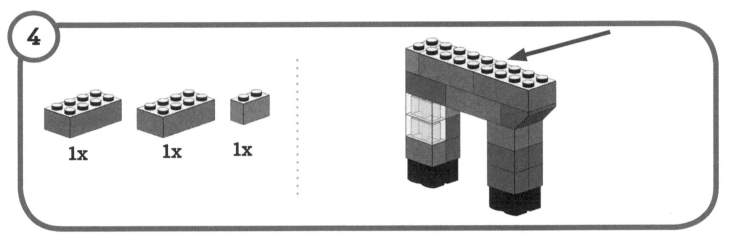

1x 1x 1x

5

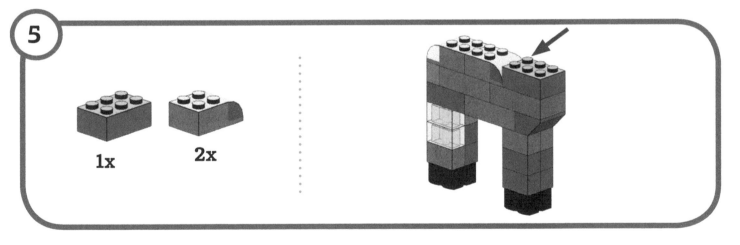

1x 2x

6

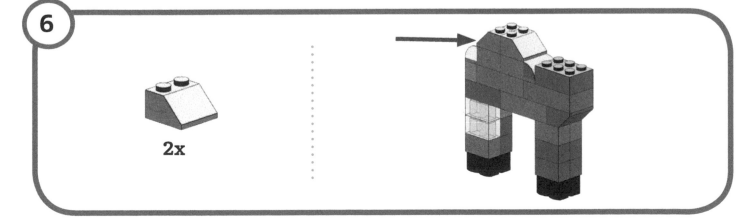

2x

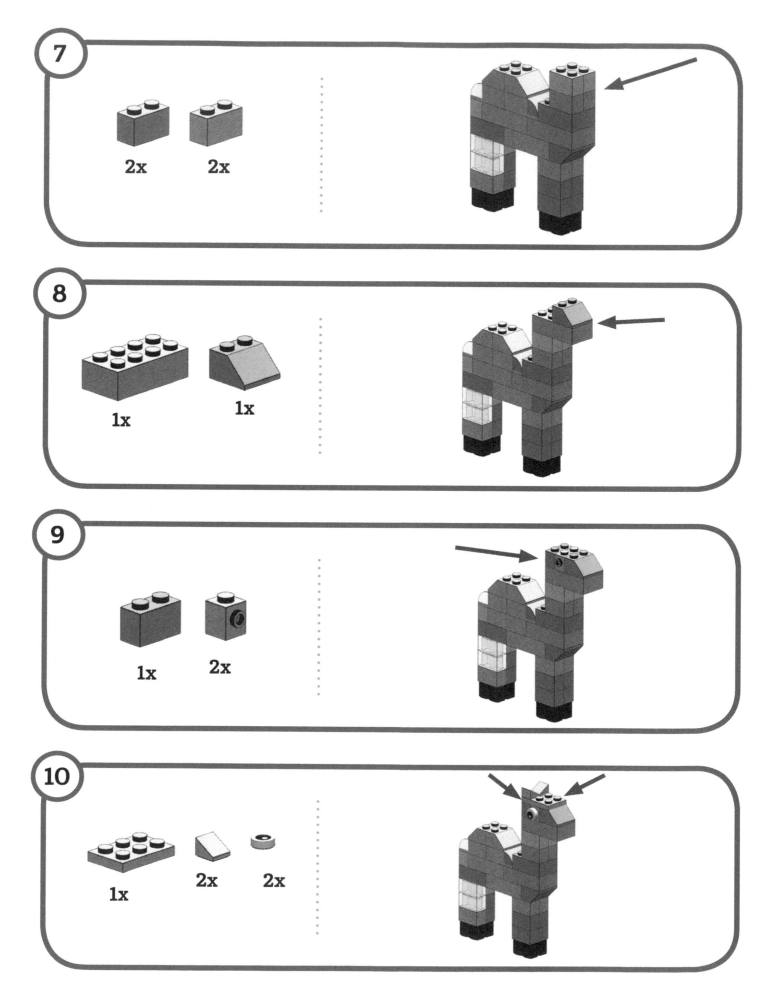

Build a Blue Cactus

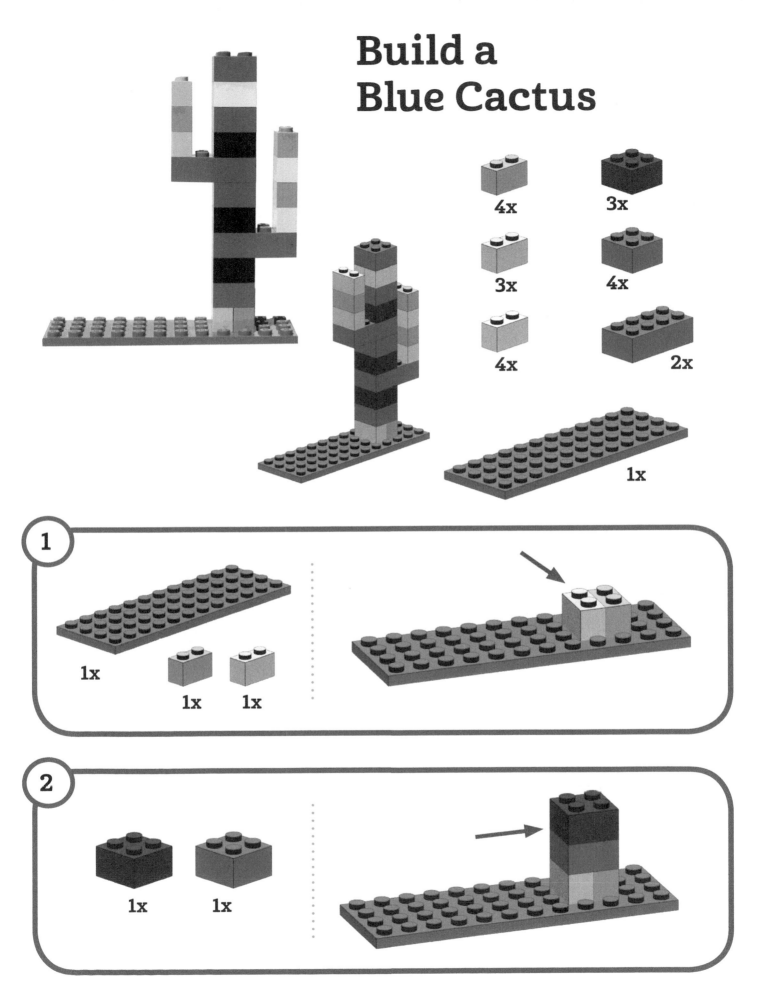

4x

3x

3x

4x

4x

2x

1x

1

1x

1x 1x

2

1x 1x

3

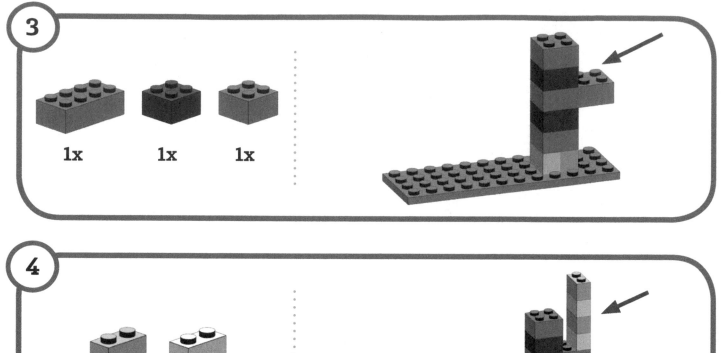

1x 1x 1x

4

2x 2x

5

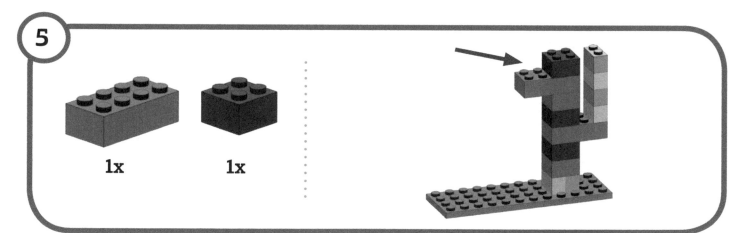

1x 1x

6

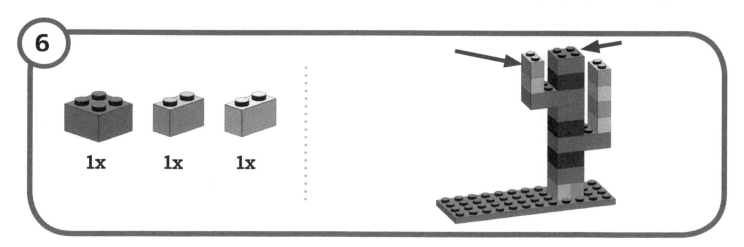

1x 1x 1x

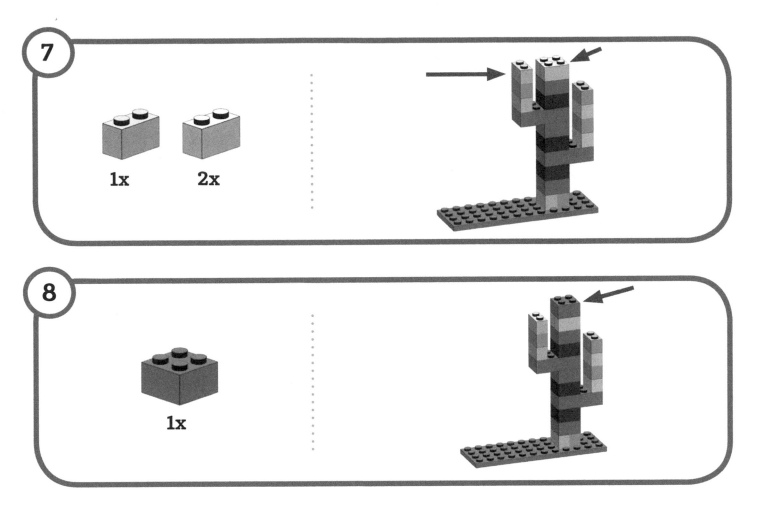

Build a Camel Calf

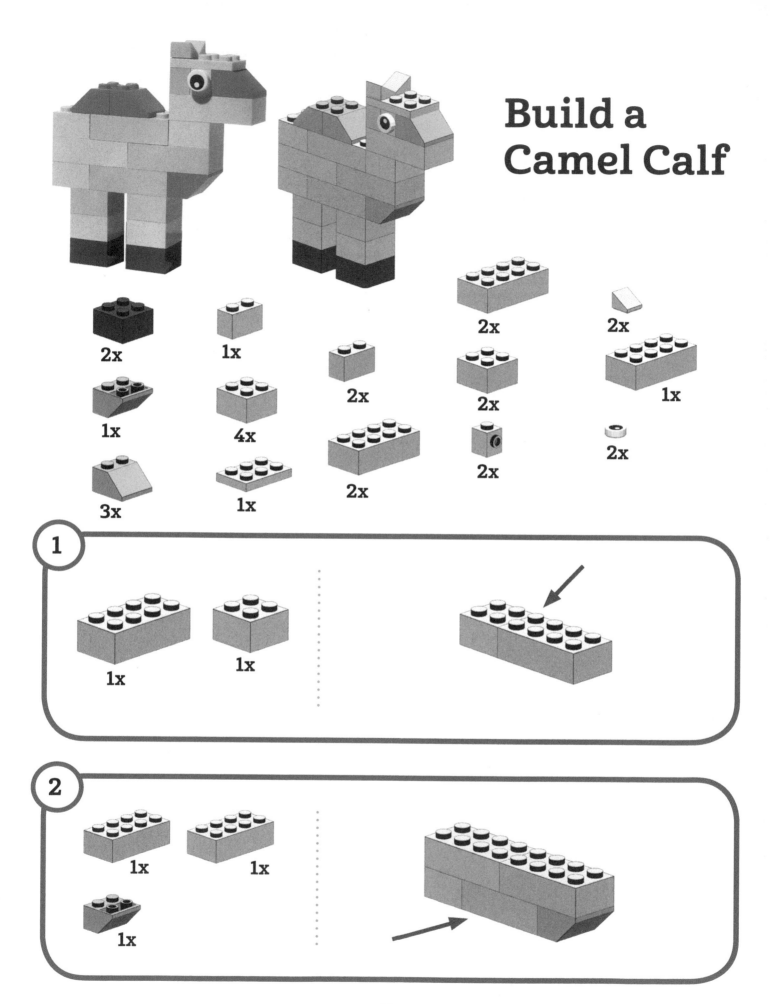

2x **1x** **2x** **2x** **2x**

1x **4x** **2x** **1x**

3x **1x** **2x** **2x** **2x**

1
1x 1x

2
1x 1x
1x

3

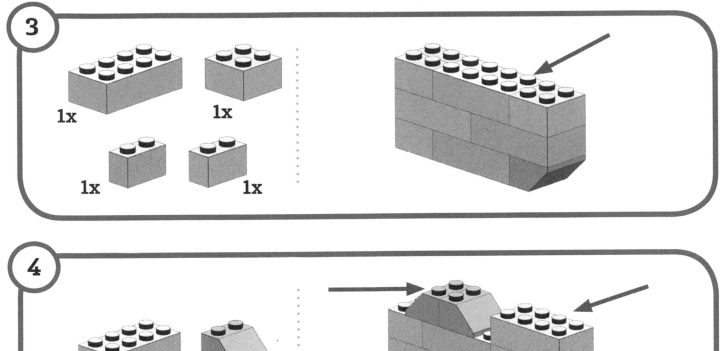

1x　　1x

1x　　1x

4

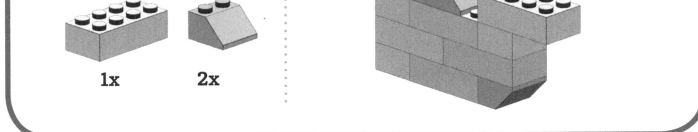

1x　　2x

5

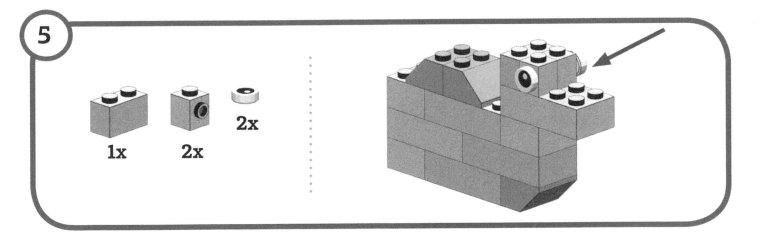

1x　　2x　　2x

6

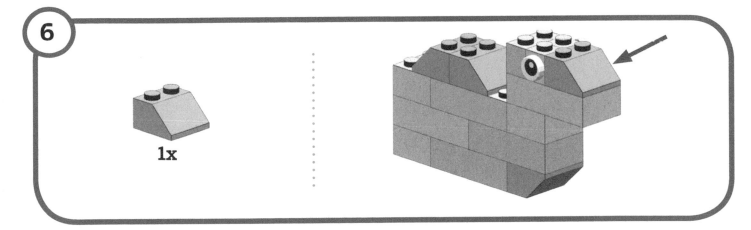

1x

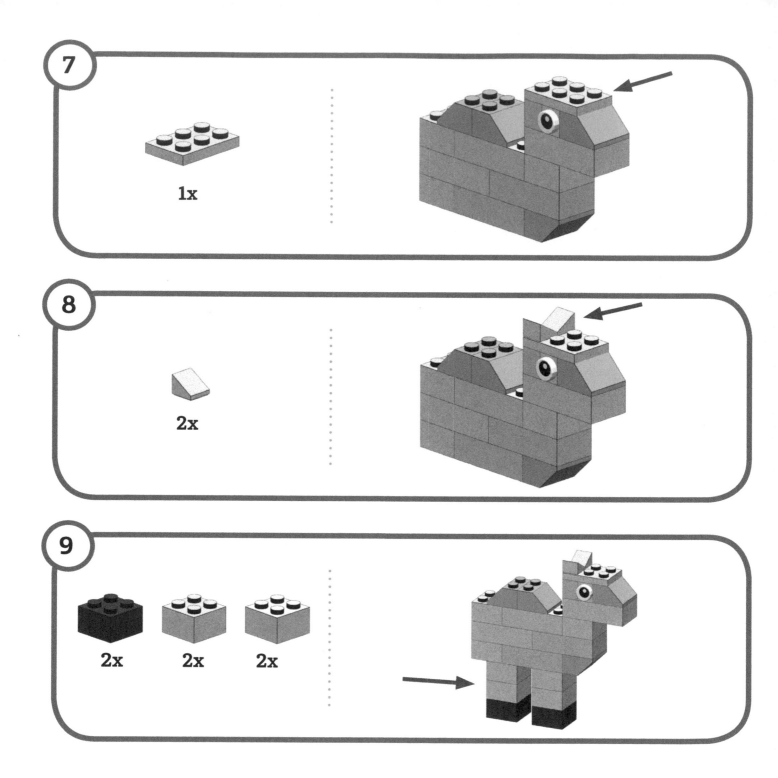

7

1x

8

2x

9

2x　2x　2x

Build a Green Cactus & Blooming Cacti

1x

4x

3x

1x

2x

3x

3x

6x

2x

4x

4x

4x

4x

4x

1x

1

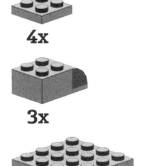

1x

1x   2x

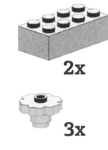

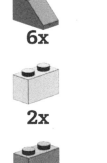

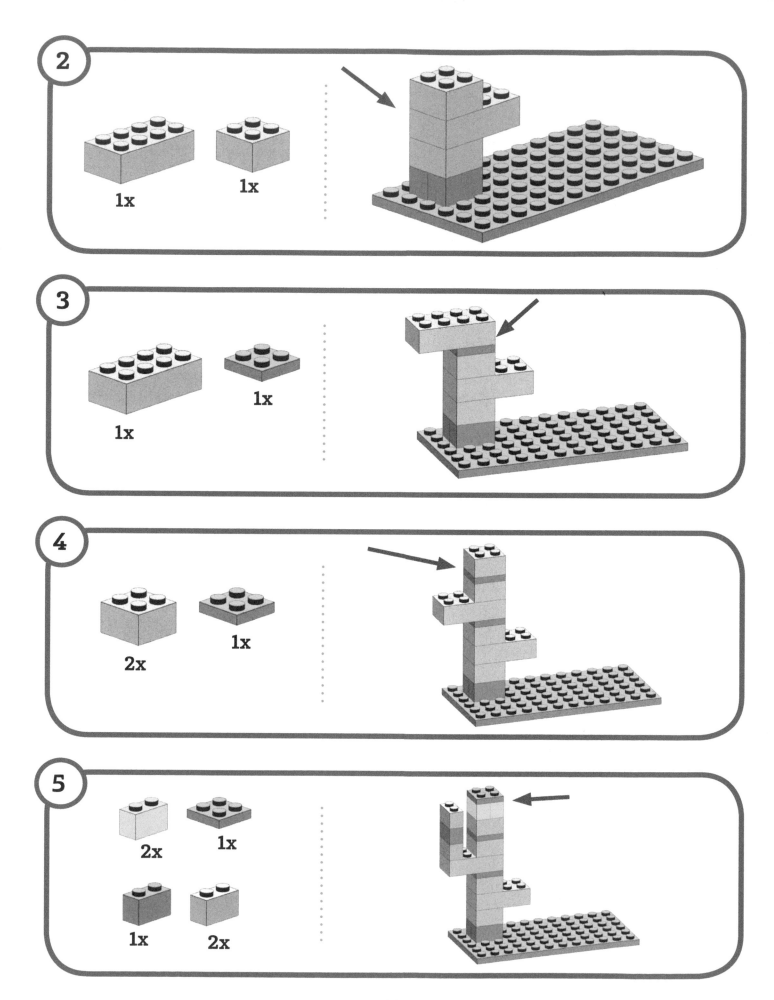

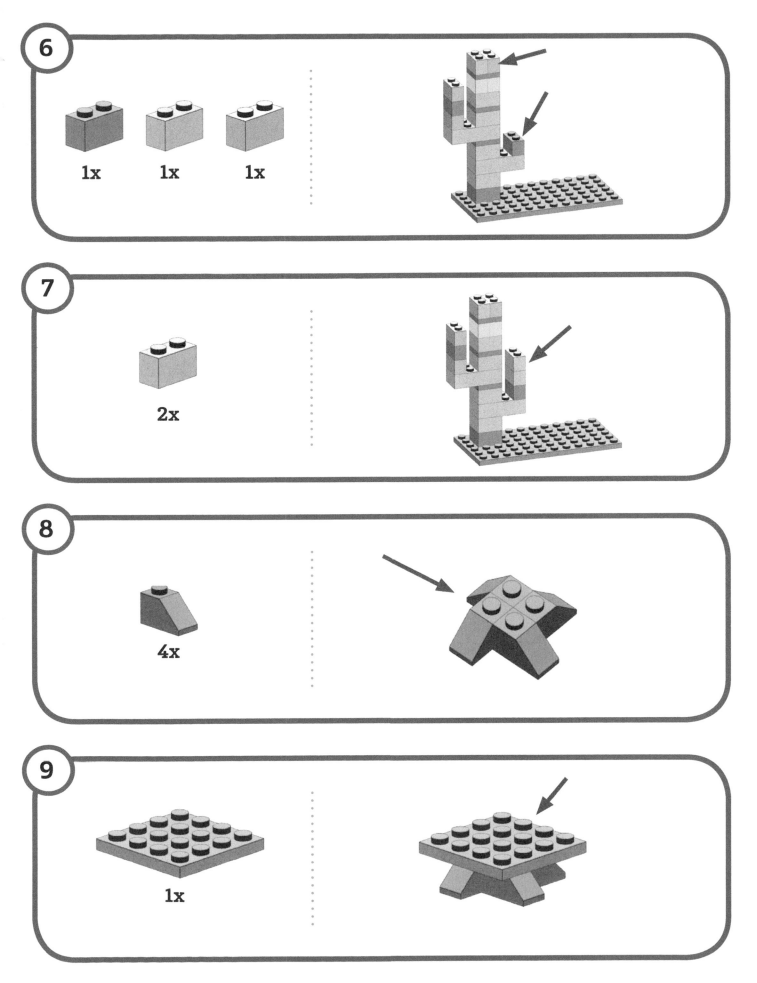

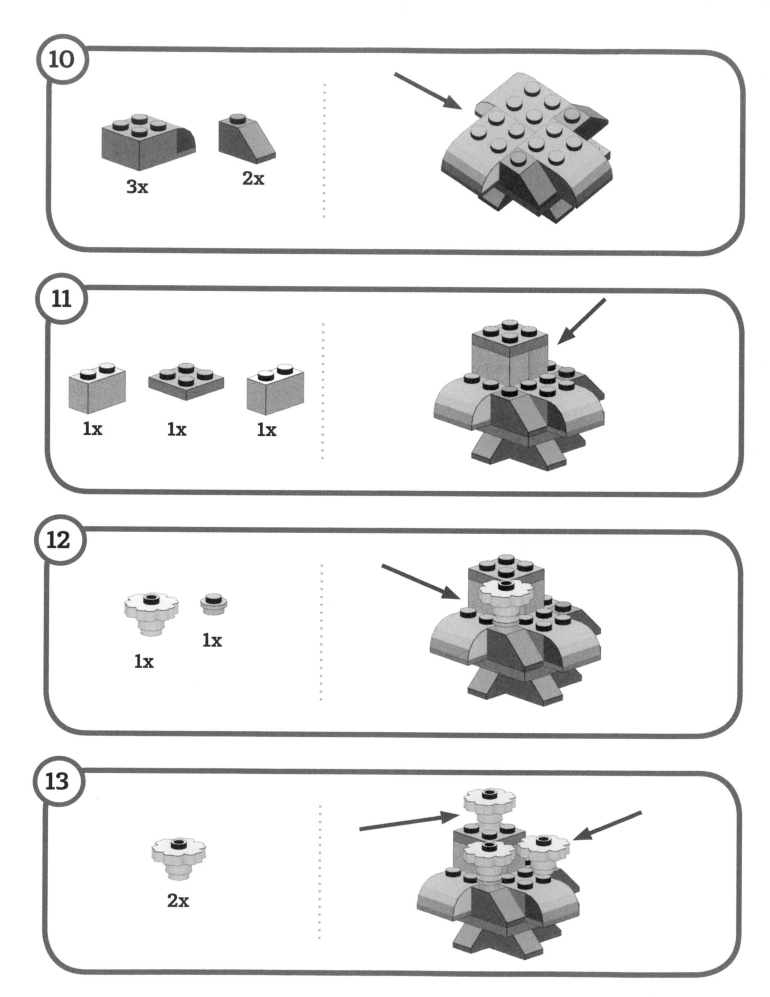

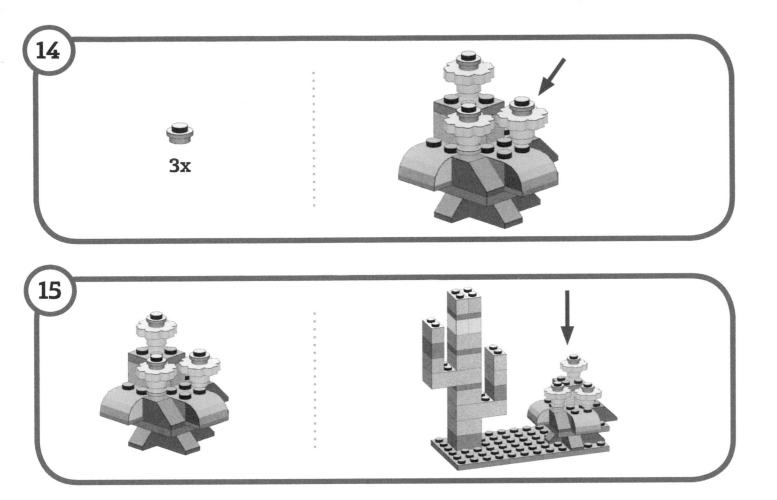

Seaside Cityscape

Helicopter

Yellow Car

Airplane

Navy Ship

Build a Navy Ship

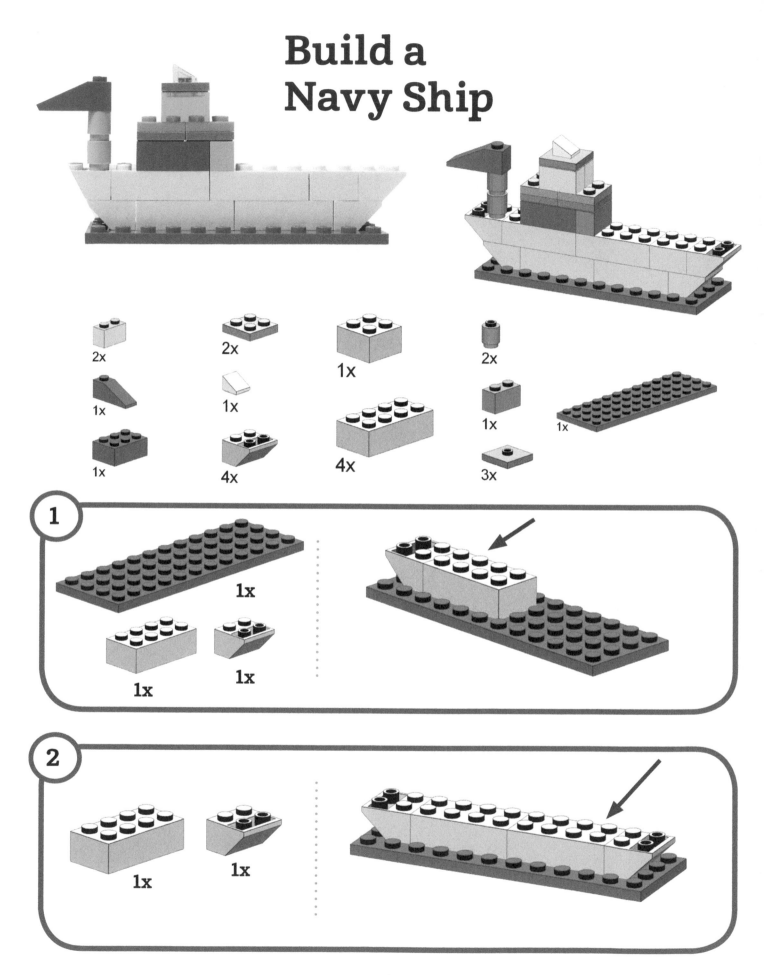

2x 2x 1x 2x

1x 1x 1x 1x

1x 4x 4x 3x

1

1x

1x 1x

2

1x 1x

3

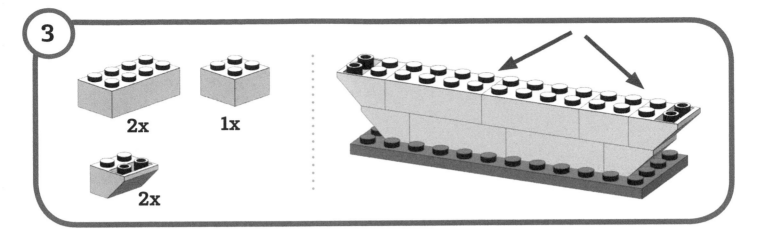

2x 1x

2x

4

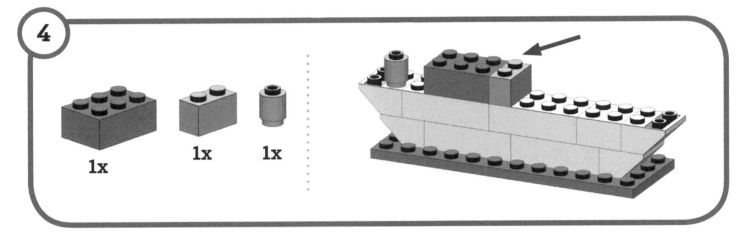

1x 1x 1x

5

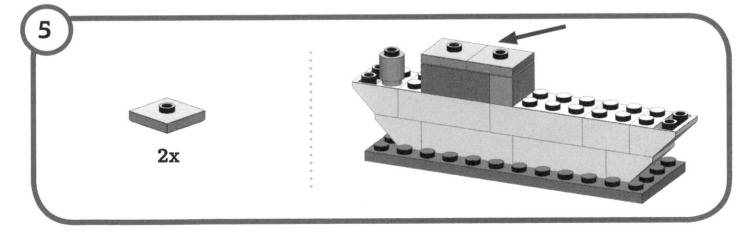

2x

6

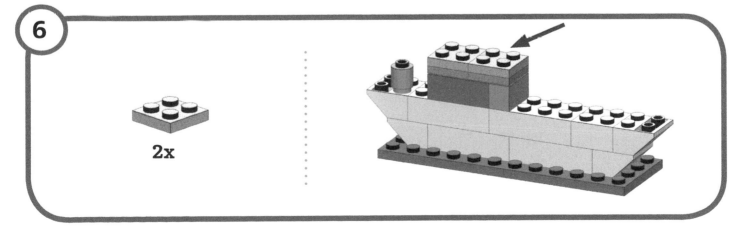

2x

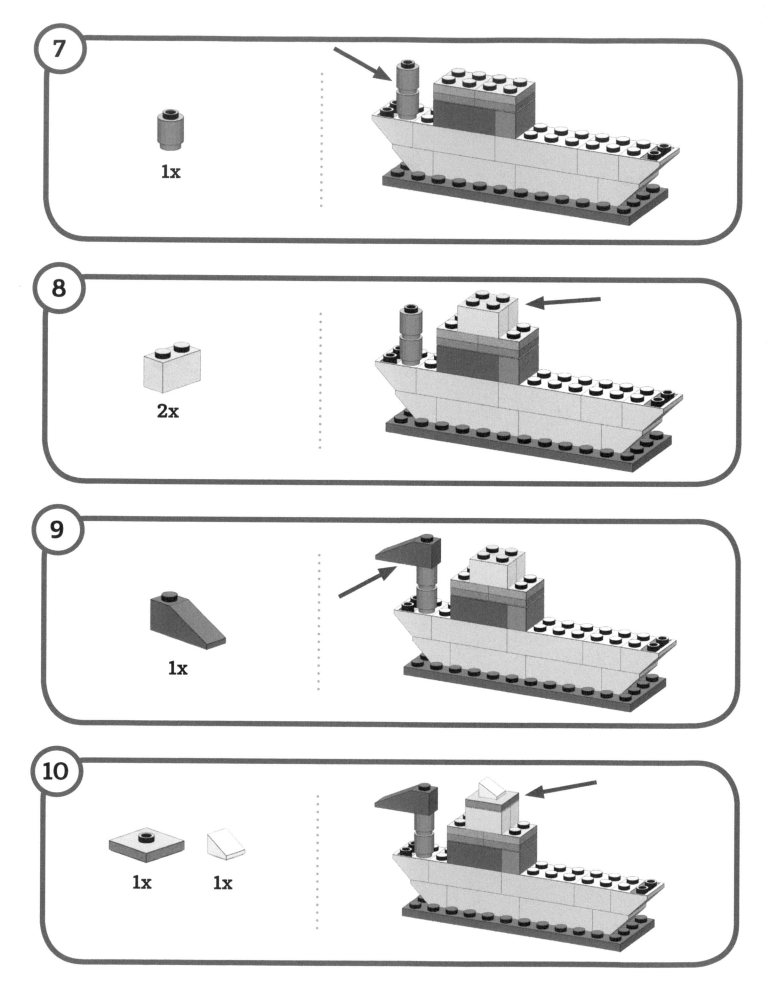

Build an
Airplane

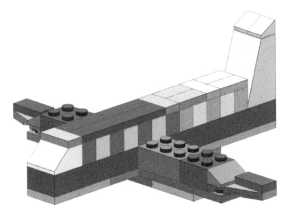

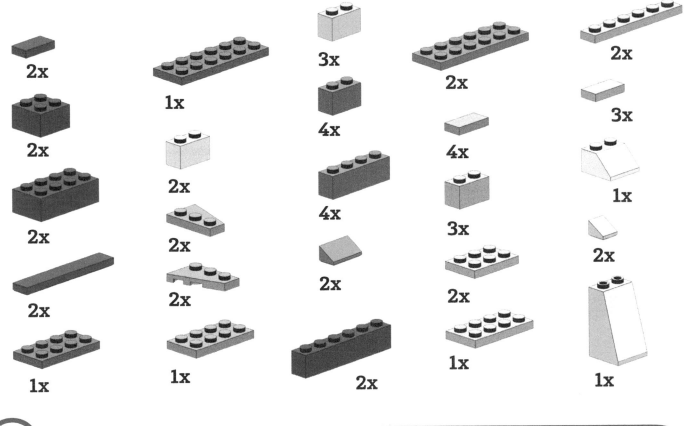

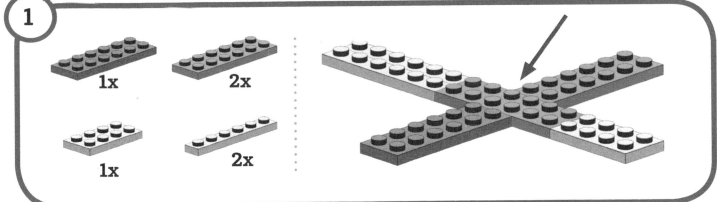

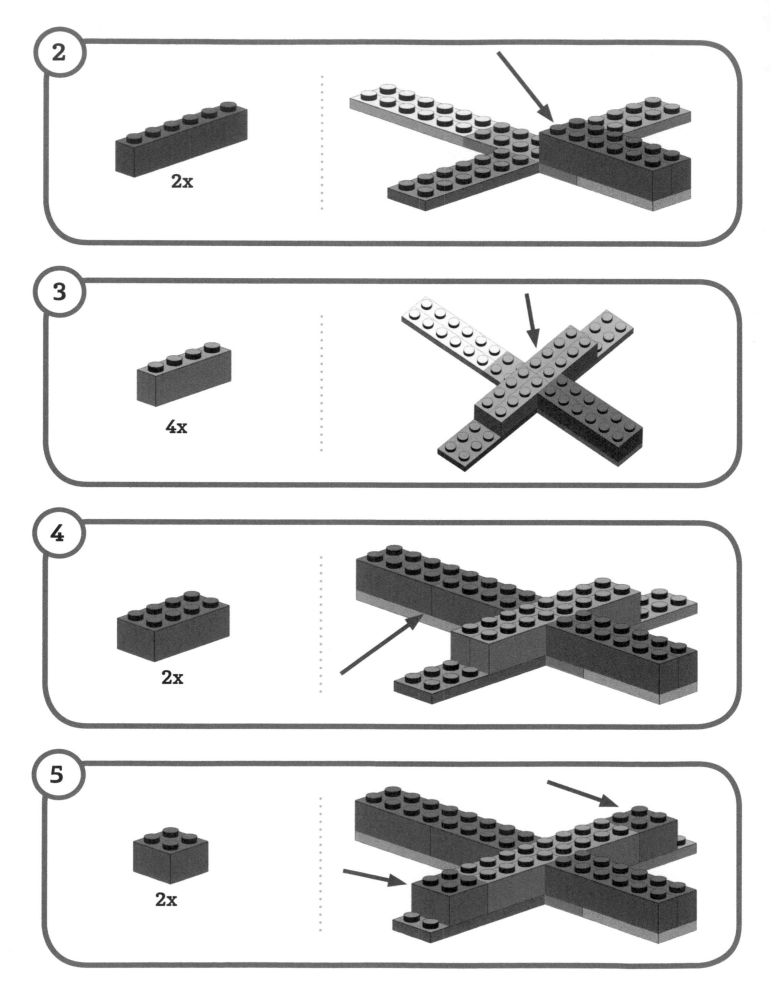

6

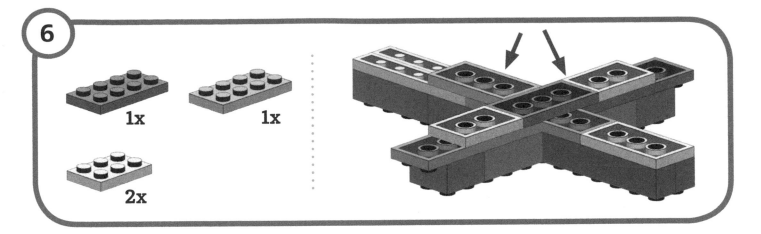

1x 1x

2x

7

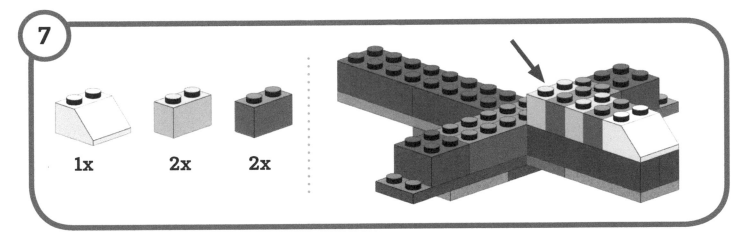

1x 2x 2x

8

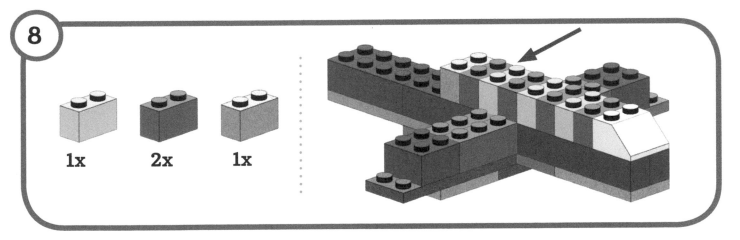

1x 2x 1x

9

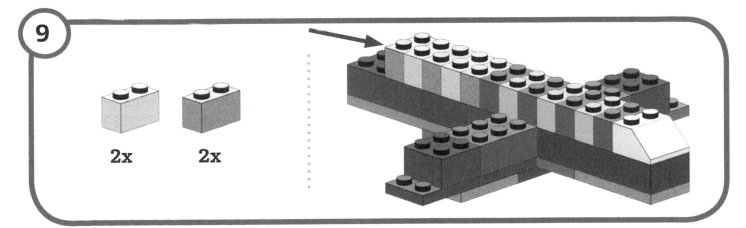

2x 2x

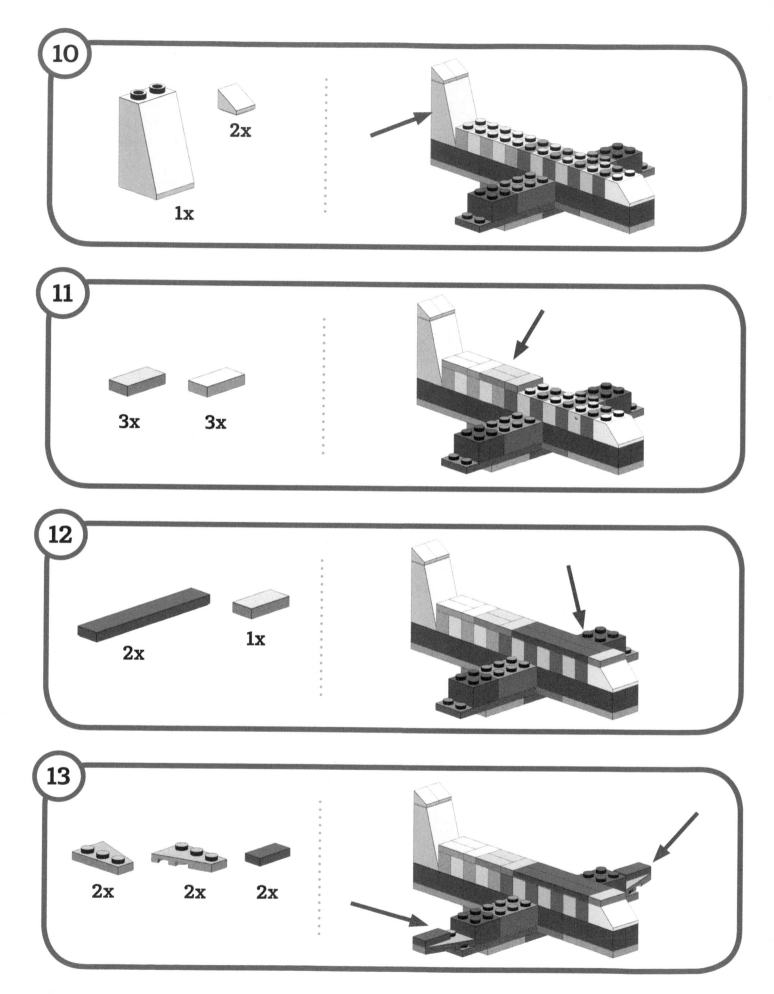

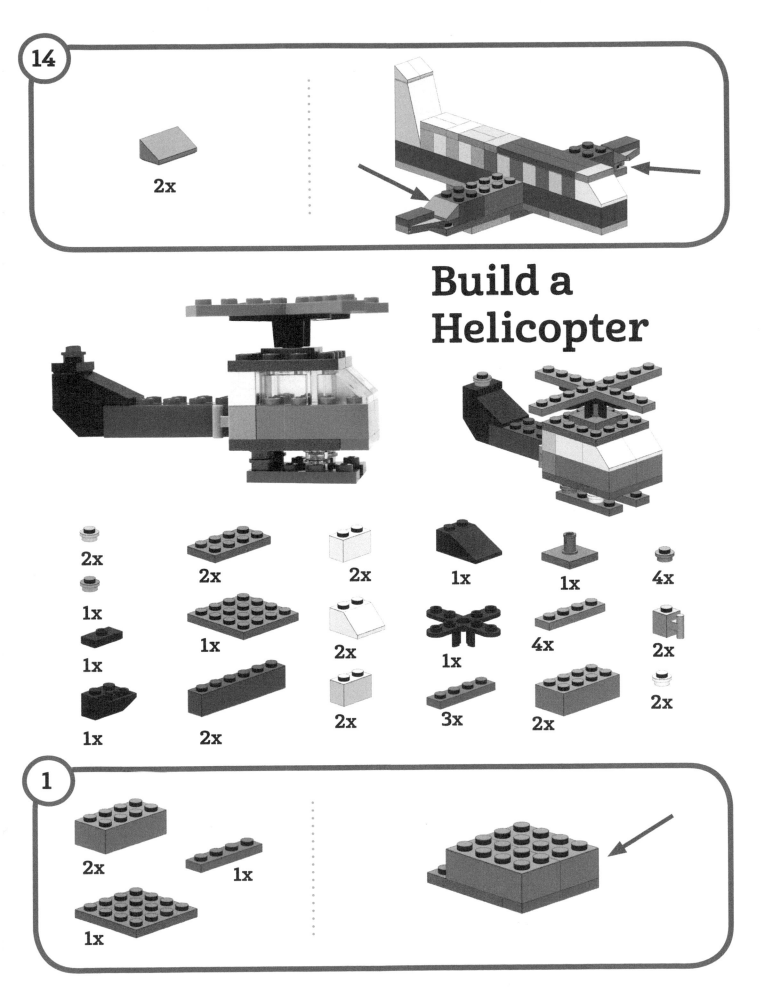

14

2x

Build a Helicopter

2x

1x

1x

2x

1x

1x

2x

1x

2x

2x

1x

2x

1x

1x

4x

1x

3x

4x

2x

2x

4x

2x

2x

1

2x

1x

1x

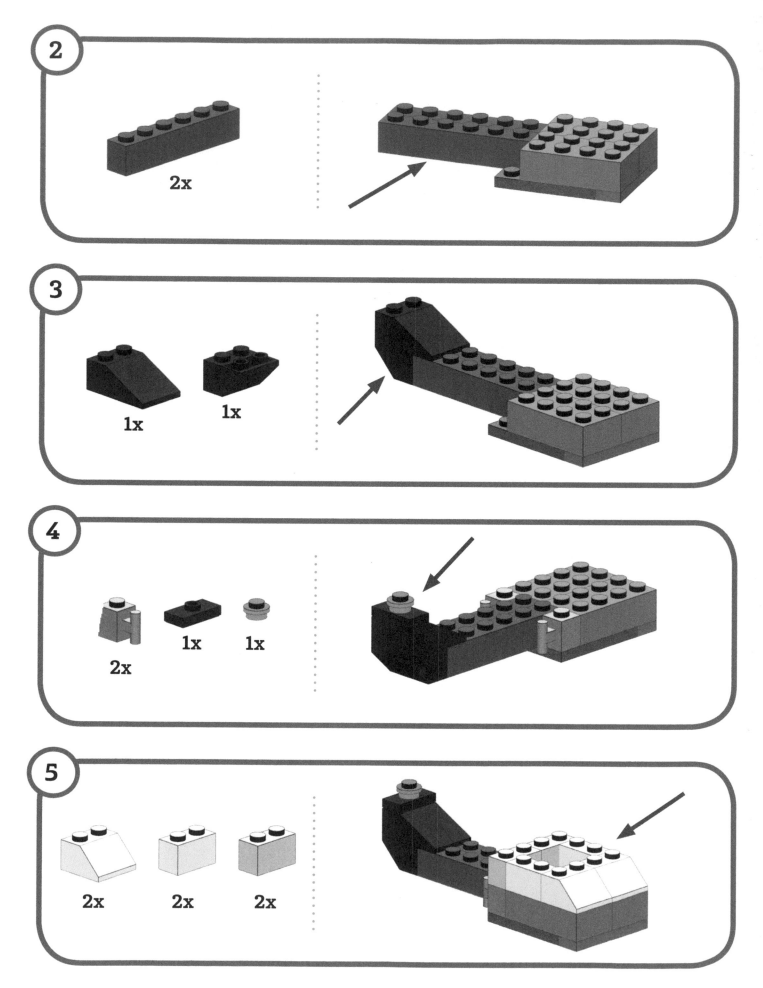

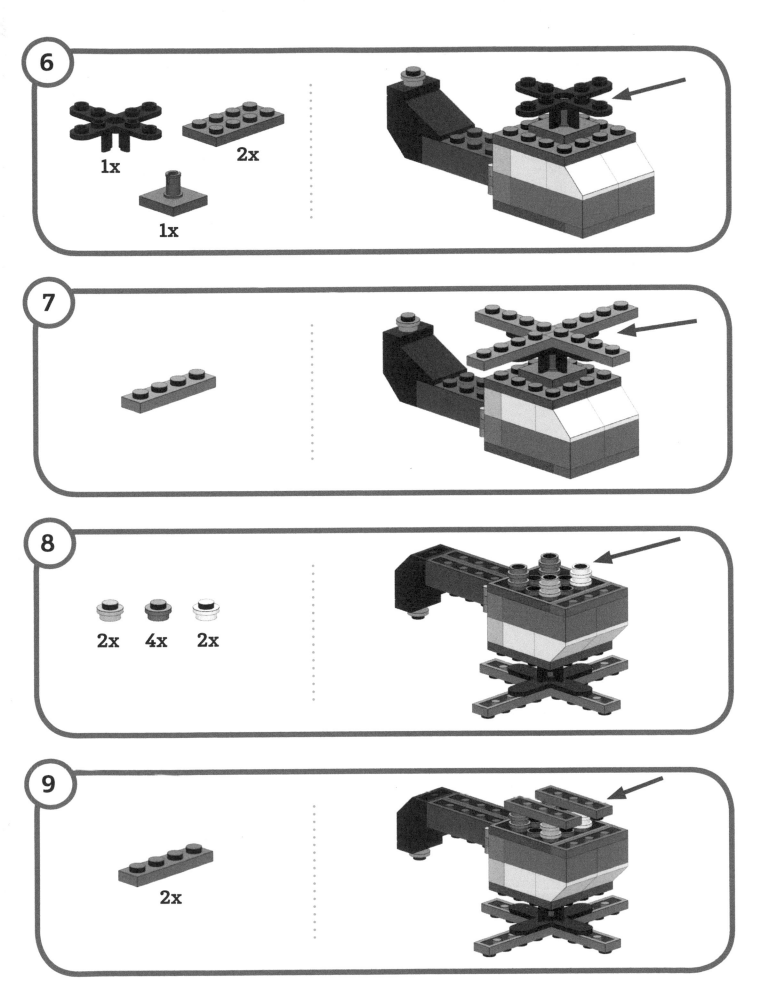

Build a Yellow Car

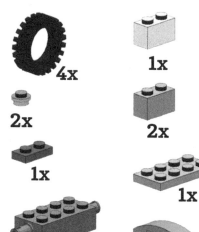

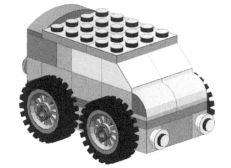

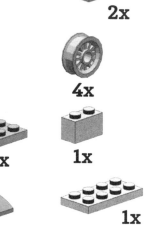

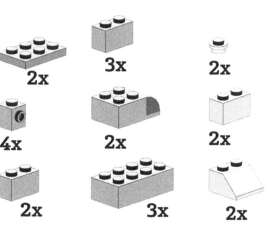

4x 1x 2x

2x 2x 4x 2x 3x 2x

1x 1x 1x 4x 2x 2x

2x 1x 1x 2x 3x 2x

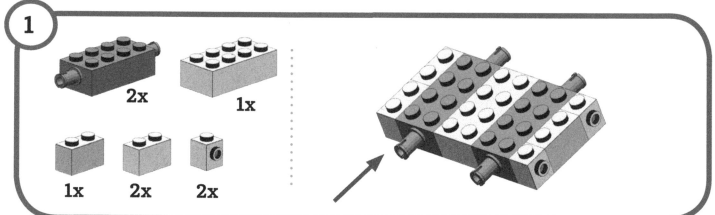

1

2x

1x

1x 2x 2x

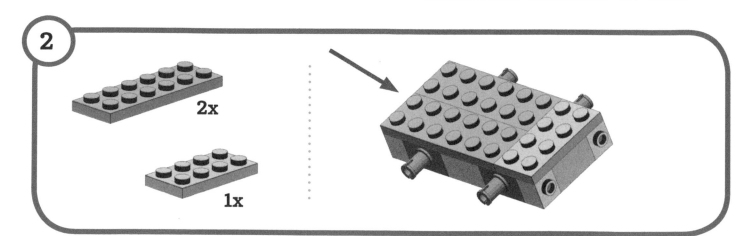

2

2x

1x

82

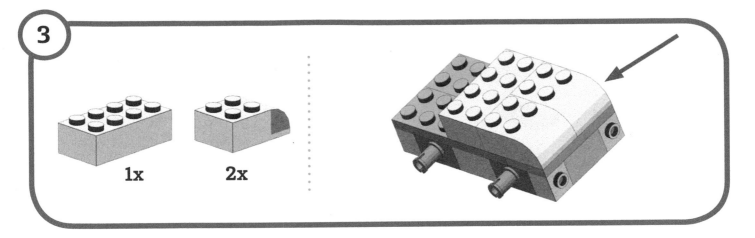

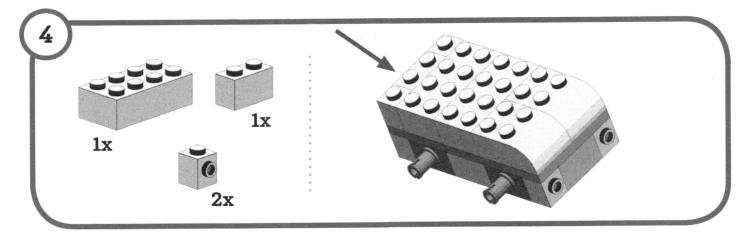

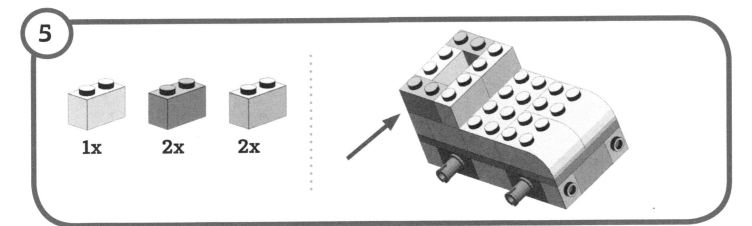

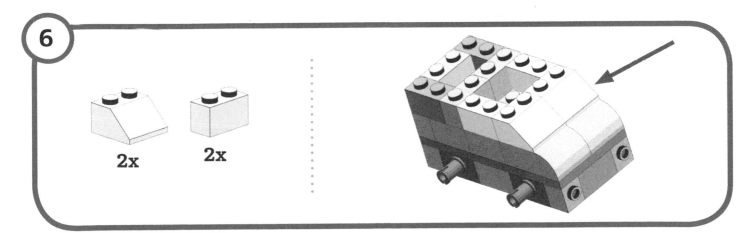

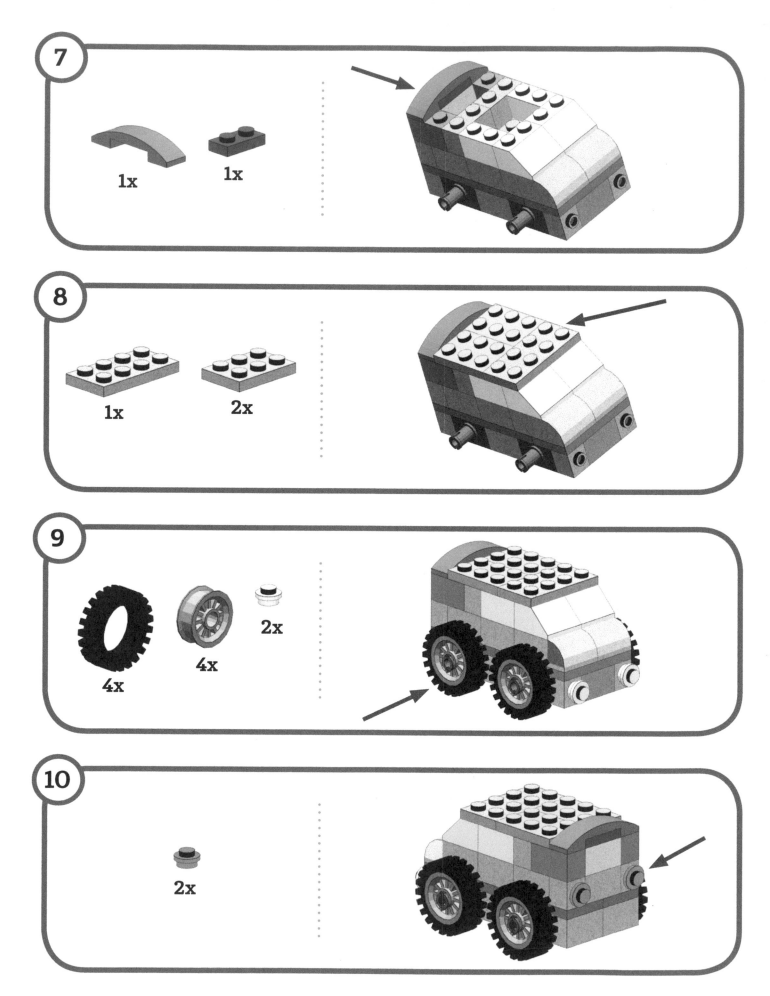

Library of Congress Control Number: 2016946780
International Standard Book Number: 978-1-943328-81-9 |
978-1-513260-39-6 (e-book) | 978-1-513260-43-3 (hardbound)
Designer: Vicki Knapton

Graphic Arts Books
An imprint of

GA

GRAPHIC ARTS
BOOKS®

P.O. Box 56118
Portland, OR 97238-6118
(503) 254-5591
www.graphicartsbooks.com

The author thanks the LDraw community for the parts database it makes available, which is used for making instructions found in the book.
For more information on LDraw, please visit ldraw.org.

CPSIA information can be obtained
at www.ICGtesting.com
Printed in the USA
BVOW11s2029151116

467961BV00002B/4/P